CAMBRIDGE
UNIVERSITY PRESS

CAMBRIDGE ENGLISH
Language Assessment
Part of the University of Cambridge

Cambridge English

CAMBRIDGE OFFICIAL PREPARATION MATERIAL

FIRST 3

WITHOUT ANSWERS

AUTHENTIC EXAMINATION PAPERS

Cambridge University Press
www.cambridge.org/elt

Cambridge Assessment English
www.cambridgeenglish.org

Information on this title: www.cambridge.org/9781108433723

First published 2018

20 19 18 17 16 15 14 13 12 11 10 9 8 7 6

Printed in Malaysia by Vivar Printing

A catalogue record for this publication is available from the British Library

ISBN 978-1-108-43373-0 Student's Book with answers
ISBN 978-1-108-38078-2 Student's Book with answers with Audio
ISBN 978-1-108-43372-3 Student's Book without answers
ISBN 978-1-108-43374-7 Audio CDs (2)

Contents

Introduction

This collection of four complete practice tests comprises papers from the *Cambridge English: First (FCE)* examination; students can practise these tests on their own or with the help of a teacher.

The *Cambridge English: First* examination is part of a suite of general English examinations produced by Cambridge English Language Assessment. This suite consists of five examinations that have similar characteristics but are designed for different levels of English language ability. Within the five levels, *Cambridge English: First* is at Level B2 in the Council of Europe's *Common European Framework of Reference for Languages: Learning, teaching, assessment.* It has also been accredited by Ofqual, the statutory regulatory authority in England, at Level 1 in the National Qualifications Framework. The *Cambridge English: First* examination is widely recognised in commerce and industry, and in individual university faculties and other educational institutions.

Examination	Council of Europe Framework Level	UK National Qualifications Framework Level
Cambridge English: Proficiency *Certificate of Proficiency in English (CPE)*	C2	3
Cambridge English: Advanced *Certificate in Advanced English (CAE)*	C1	2
Cambridge English: First *First Certificate in English (FCE)*	B2	1
Cambridge English: Preliminary *Preliminary English Test (PET)*	B1	Entry 3
Cambridge English: Key *Key English Test (KET)*	A2	Entry 2

Further information

The information contained in this practice book is designed to be an overview of the exam. For a full description of all of the above exams, including information about task types, testing focus and preparation, please see the relevant handbooks which can be obtained from Cambridge English Language Assessment at the address below or from the website at: www.CambridgeEnglish.org

Cambridge English Language Assessment
1 Hills Road
Cambridge CB1 2EU
United Kingdom

Telephone: +44 1223 553997
email: helpdesk@cambridgeenglish.org

The structure of *Cambridge English: First* – an overview

The *Cambridge English: First* examination consists of four papers.

Reading and Use of English 1 hour 15 minutes
This paper consists of **seven parts**, with 52 questions. For Parts 1 to 4, the test contains texts with accompanying grammar and vocabulary tasks, and separate items with a grammar and vocabulary focus. For Parts 5 to 7, the test contains a range of texts and accompanying reading comprehension tasks.

Writing 1 hour 20 minutes
This paper consists of **two parts** which carry equal marks. In Part 1, which is **compulsory**, candidates have to write an essay of between 140 and 190 words, giving their opinion in response to a task. In Part 2, there are three tasks from which candidates choose one to write about. The range of tasks from which questions may be drawn includes an article, an email/letter, a report and a review. In this part, candidates have to write between 140 and 190 words.

Listening 40 minutes (approximately)
This paper consists of **four parts**. Each part contains a recorded text or texts and some questions, including multiple-choice, sentence completion and multiple-matching questions. Each text is heard twice. There is a total of **30 questions**.

Speaking 14 minutes
This paper consists of **four parts**. The standard test format is two candidates and two examiners. One examiner takes part in the conversation while the other examiner listens. Both examiners give marks. Candidates will be given photographs and other visual and written material to look at and talk about. Sometimes candidates will talk with the other candidate, sometimes with the examiner, and sometimes with both.

Grading

Candidates will receive a score on the Cambridge English Scale for each of the four skills and Use of English. The average of these five scores gives the candidate's overall Cambridge English Scale score for the exam. This determines what grade and CEFR level they achieve. All candidates receive a Statement of Results and candidates who pass the examination with Grade A, B or C also receive the *First Certificate in English*. Candidates who achieve Grade A receive the *First Certificate in English* stating that they demonstrated ability at Level C1. Candidates who achieve Grade B or C receive the *First Certificate in English* certificate stating that they demonstrated ability at Level B2. Candidates whose performance is below B2 level, but falls within Level B1, receive a *Cambridge English* certificate stating that they have demonstrated ability at Level B1. Candidates whose performance falls below Level B1 do not receive a certificate.

For further information on grading and results, go to the website (see page 4).

Test 1

READING AND USE OF ENGLISH (1 hour 15 minutes)

Part 1

For questions **1–8**, read the text below and decide which answer (**A**, **B**, **C** or **D**) best fits each gap. There is an example at the beginning (**0**).

Mark your answers **on the separate answer sheet**.

Example:

0 **A** gather **B** produce **C** find **D** gain

0	A	B	C	D
	▭	▭	▭	▬

Alfred Wainwright

Alfred Wainwright came from a relatively poor family but managed to **(0)** .... qualifications in accountancy. However it is not for his skill in accountancy that he is **(1)** .... but for his pictorial guidebooks to the English Lake District.

The Lake District is in the north-west of England and **(2)** .... an area of some 2,292 square kilometres. As its name **(3)** .... , it is an area of lakes and mountains. Alfred first went there on a walking holiday in 1930 and immediately fell in love with the area.

He **(4)** .... the Lake District into seven parts and wrote a guide for each of them. The guides **(5)** .... entirely of copies of his hand-written manuscripts. All have descriptions of walks with hand-drawn maps and sketches of views from the summits of the different mountains. He intended the books to be just for his own personal **(6)** .... but was eventually **(7)** .... to publish them. They are beautiful books which **(8)** .... as popular as ever.

1	**A**	reminded	**B**	recollected	**C**	referred	**D**	remembered
2	**A**	reaches	**B**	extends	**C**	ranges	**D**	covers
3	**A**	implies	**B**	represents	**C**	proves	**D**	means
4	**A**	distributed	**B**	assigned	**C**	divided	**D**	allocated
5	**A**	involve	**B**	consist	**C**	include	**D**	contain
6	**A**	application	**B**	use	**C**	employment	**D**	practice
7	**A**	persuaded	**B**	impressed	**C**	caused	**D**	influenced
8	**A**	stay	**B**	keep	**C**	continue	**D**	remain

Part 2

For questions **9–16**, read the text below and think of the word which best fits each gap. Use only **one** word in each gap. There is an example at the beginning (**0**).

Write your answers **IN CAPITAL LETTERS on the separate answer sheet**.

Example: | 0 | T | O |

The origin of coins

According **(0)** .... the Greek historian Herodotus (484–425 BC), the Lydian people were the first to use metallic coins. In fact, these earliest coins were made out **(9)** .... electrum, a naturally-occurring mixture of gold and silver. The coins were first produced in the seventh century BC with a design on **(10)** .... side only; the other was marked with simple punches. Each coin was assigned a value in units. Some coins were inscribed with names in Lydian script, but it is unclear **(11)** .... these are names of kings or just of rich men who produced the coins. **(12)** .... of the irregular size and shape of the coins, it must **(13)** .... been difficult to tell one **(14)** .... another, especially some of the smaller ones. Thus, many costs were expressed **(15)** .... terms of the total weight of the coins required and transactions were completed by weighing the coins used together, **(16)** .... than counting individual ones.

Part 3

For questions **17–24**, read the text below. Use the word given in capitals at the end of some of the lines to form a word that fits in the gap **in the same line**. There is an example at the beginning (**0**).

Write your answers **IN CAPITAL LETTERS on the separate answer sheet**.

Example: | 0 | A C T I V I T Y |

Play

Play is an **(0)** .... that all children take part in, whether alone or with	**ACTIVE**
others. In fact, play offers a wide **(17)** .... of benefits for children	**VARY**
and is vital for a child's learning and **(18)** .... development. It	**EMOTION**
is central to the formation of a child's personality and can help to	
increase the knowledge children need to cope with the challenges	
they encounter in school and at home. Play enables children to realise	
their potential and to find solutions to problems, thus allowing them to	
experience the **(19)** .... that success brings.	**SATISFY**
Experts tell us that it is **(20)** .... to overestimate the	**POSSIBLE**
(21) .... of play as it is probably the most effective way that	**IMPORTANT**
children have of trying out and mastering new skills. By opening	
children's minds to **(22)** .... and imagination, play is indeed a good	**CREATE**
(23) .... for life.	**PREPARE**
However, as far as children themselves are concerned, the only value	
of play is quite simply in the fun and **(24)** .... that it gives them.	**PLEASE**

Part 4

For questions **25–30**, complete the second sentence so that it has a similar meaning to the first sentence, using the word given. **Do not change the word given**. You must use between **two** and **five** words, including the word given. Here is an example (**0**).

Example:

0 A very friendly taxi driver drove us into town.

DRIVEN

We .... a very friendly taxi driver.

The gap can be filled by the words 'were driven into town by', so you write:

Example:	**0**	*WERE DRIVEN INTO TOWN BY*

Write **only** the missing words **IN CAPITAL LETTERS on the separate answer sheet**.

---

25 Martin never goes to bed without having a shower first.

HAS

Martin always .... to bed.

26 Tina was too frightened to stay in the house on her own.

BEEN

Tina would have stayed in the house on her own .... so frightened.

27 It will not be possible to buy tickets for the match until next Monday.

SALE

Tickets for the match will .... until next Monday.

28 The only vegetable that Helen dislikes is cabbage.

VEGETABLES

Helen .... from cabbages.

29 When Alex has finished his essay, a friend is going to check the spelling for him.

CHECKED

When Alex has finished his essay, he is going to .... a friend.

30 'I'm sorry to disturb you when you're so busy,' said Tom.

EXCUSE

'Please .... you when you're so busy,' said Tom.

Part 5

You are going to read part of the introduction to a cookery book called *In Search of Total Perfection* by Heston Blumenthal. For questions **31–36**, choose the answer (**A**, **B**, **C** or **D**) which you think fits best according to the text.

Mark your answers **on the separate answer sheet**.

When my first cookery programme *In Search of Perfection* first came out, I had no idea how it would be received by the viewers and the press. There had been plenty of talk going round at the time about the food 'revolution' sweeping through Britain, and I was certain that we'd produced a series of programmes that made a genuinely innovative contribution to that, but still the question worried me: would people appreciate an approach to cooking that involved not just techniques but also history, nostalgia and science? I watched the first programme in a mixed state of joy and fear.

I needn't have worried. The subsequent success of the show paved the way for all sorts of other fascinating projects, including a book based on my experiences at the restaurant I own. In each project there is a sense of being on a journey, be it into the past, into the mind, or into cookery techniques. I then wrote several books in a series called 'Perfection', each one accompanying its own TV programme of the same name. In these, however, the journey was often a very physical one, with passports and suitcases and itineraries. *In Search of Total Perfection* is the latest in the series, and in it you'll zigzag the globe in order to meet some extraordinary artisans, such as a man who finds his true purpose in creating a golden pasta that tastes better than any other. These people have spent decades pursuing their own ideals of perfection.

Perfection is, of course, highly subjective. Even the seemingly simple task of choosing which dishes to include in the series turned out to be a nightmare, and I knew I was bound to upset many people by leaving out their particular favourite. 'Where's steak and kidney pie and bread and butter pudding?' I could imagine people saying. Nevertheless, after shutting ourselves away in a meeting room and agreeing not to emerge until we had come up with a suitable list, the TV production team and I eventually had something for everyone.

This reinforced my opinion that each of us has our own idea of what constitutes perfection, drawing heavily on a highly personalised mix of emotions, memories and surroundings. Despite the book's title, *In Search of Perfection*, I knew from the outset that I wouldn't be claiming the recipes were in any way 'definitive'. But I reckoned that, by using my technical skill and scientific knowledge, by talking to food producers and artisans and chefs and their customers, I could pin down some of the things that made these dishes work.

While the dictionary defines 'perfection' as the state of being perfect, it also offers a second definition of equal importance to this book: honing through gradual experimentation. *line 62* Trying out ideas and then revising them until you arrive at something uniquely wonderful. The TV series gave me the opportunity to get out and look into all sorts of foods, people and places I'd never encountered before in any restaurant, and I was as excited about that as I *line 68* was about the chance to explore memory and nostalgia in food because I started out in this business in exactly the same way.

Searching out the best ingredients for the recipes took me all over the globe. Among my adventures were: being taken with great solemnity and assurance to a canning factory that turned out to be processing completely the wrong sort of tomato, and visiting a dairy farm whose standards fell so far short of perfection that we had to stop filming there! Refining the technique for each recipe, I ended up hand-milking a cow and then using dry ice to turn the milk into ice cream, cooking chicken breasts in a hospital scanning machine and nearly burning my house down in an effort to get the oven hot enough for a proper Neapolitan-style pizza.

31 In the second paragraph, Heston implies that the books in the 'Perfection' series

- **A** had a more international focus than his first book.
- **B** strongly developed the psychological aspect of the subject.
- **C** feature some characters who re-appeared in different books.
- **D** were less successful than the TV programmes that went with them.

32 What did Heston think about the meeting to discuss the 'Perfection' series?

- **A** It was useful in highlighting some practical problems.
- **B** It resulted in a very strange decision.
- **C** It should have been more productive.
- **D** It was demanding but efficient.

33 What does Heston imply about the recipes in his new book?

- **A** They vary considerably from the versions that inspired them.
- **B** They could be developed further in the future.
- **C** The final wording of them was easy to come up with.
- **D** The selection is not necessarily one he would have made himself.

34 What does 'honing' in line 62 tell us about the recipes?

- **A** They can never be completely perfect.
- **B** They are regarded by Heston as being experimental.
- **C** They serve another significant purpose in Heston's book.
- **D** They have been worked on and improved over a period of time.

35 What does 'that' refer to in line 68?

- **A** being willing to try out new things
- **B** learning the trade in a particular restaurant
- **C** exploring the relationship between food and the past
- **D** wondering about the importance of food in people's lives

36 Heston says that during his travels around the globe, he

- **A** had to be resourceful and adaptable.
- **B** narrowly avoided disaster on several occasions.
- **C** was forever solving problems caused by other people's incompetence.
- **D** had to respect an unusual local custom.

Part 6

You are going to a read a newspaper article about observing marine creatures called manatees. Six sentences have been removed from the article. Choose from the sentences **A–G** the one which fits each gap (**37–42**). There is one extra sentence which you do not need to use.

Mark your answers **on the separate answer sheet.**

Swimming with Manatees, Florida's Gentle Giants

When most people flock to the famous amusement parks in Orlando, Florida, they miss some of the natural wonders the State has to offer. It was in Citrus County on the beautiful west coast of Florida that we went to see the manatee, an amazing mammal that occupies coastal waters and rivers.

Our days started early in the morning at Homosassa Springs, as this is the perfect time to snorkel with the manatees before they get tired of visitors. We boarded a pontoon boat with Captain Traci Wood from Native Vacations. Having spotted two manatees just below the water, Captain Traci stopped the boat as the duo slowly glided towards us. **37** ____ Our boat was soon surrounded by other members of this gentle species.

Soon we resumed our journey. Within a few minutes Captain Traci stopped the boat again and we were given instructions. Whatever you do, she said, remember the three golden rules: minimize splash noise; act with very slow movements; and when you touch one of these friendly, gentle gray giants on the back or stomach, never touch with more than one hand at a time. The Endangered Species Act forbids touching a manatee unless it touches you first, and they will let you know. The protection of this endangered species is taken very seriously. For children, there is absolutely no chasing or riding the manatees. **38** ____ Most Homosassa manatees are very social and will come to you.

The next day, at Three Sisters Springs, we entered the water very slowly, trying to keep down the amount of thick, muddy sediment rising from the bottom of the river. **39** ____ This meant swimming with the manatees was not at all difficult or intimidating. We saw young children as well as seniors in the water and there was an abundant feeling of energy and curiosity among us all.

Manatees are strictly herbivores, and they eat a great variety of species, including water hyacinth and water lettuce. They're very big, measuring 3 to 5 metres and weighing as much as 1,600 kilos. **40** ____ Manatees are of course wild creatures, although when face to face with them, you're unlikely to feel any fear.

Since not all visitors want to get nose-to-nose with the manatees, non-swimmers can also view them at Homosassa Springs State Wildlife Park. The park provides a wonderful home for some manatees **41** ____ They are well looked after by people who really understand them. The park also serves as a research and observation center, offering three daily educational programs to the public.

From December to March, groups of manatees escape the cold winter ocean and bask in the warm waters near power plants and coastal springs that stay about 23 degrees year-round. Snorkelers, divers and swimmers come to Florida from all over the world for a chance to swim or interact with the docile manatee in its natural environment, rich in marine vegetation. **42** ____ So the manatees arrive every year by the hundreds to find warmth, nourishment and maybe, just maybe, to visit us, the curious humans.

A The truth is, swimming with manatees is a life-altering experience.

B Those that have been injured or orphaned will also spend their lives there since they are unable to survive in the wild.

C But this won't diminish the experience in the least.

D This abundant source of food makes this area an ideal habitat for the manatees.

E This was to avoid disturbing some of the manatees who were still sleeping while others were slow-paddling around.

F They used their paddle-like tails to propel themselves, steering with their flippers, gracefully moving their bodies through the water in our direction.

G Despite this, they look very cute.

Part 7

You are going to read an article about four people who set up local environmental projects. For questions **43–52**, choose from the people (**A–D**). The people may be chosen more than once.

Mark your answers **on the separate answer sheet**.

Which person

accepted that the attitudes of local people might be impossible to change?	**43**	
included a useful additional feature on a product?	**44**	
co-operated with others to develop the initial idea?	**45**	
had to convince local people to take part in an experiment?	**46**	
managed to get products sold in other countries?	**47**	
received formal recognition for a project's achievements?	**48**	
realised that it wasn't possible to use ideas that had worked elsewhere?	**49**	
saw that a traditional way of life was under threat?	**50**	
created an example that people in different places were able to follow?	**51**	
used materials that they recycled?	**52**	

Local environmental heroes

Four innovators who founded local conservation projects

A Evans Wadongo

Like many Kenyans, Evans Wadongo grew up studying by the light of a kerosene lamp. Bad for his eyes, the lamps also produced harmful fumes that made him cough. So, Evans designed a cleaner sun-powered alternative. Instead of importing solar technology from a mass-producing country, he set up the Use Solar initiative, which trained youngsters to manufacture special solar-powered lamps, using locally-sourced scrap metal and fragments of solar panels. A USB port, built into the base, offered an easy way to charge phones and radios. The lamps were then given to local groups, who used the money they saved on kerosene to set up small businesses such as poultry farming or beekeeping. Evans says that getting finance for the project was a challenge due to its long-term nature. Each lamp costs $25, which covers materials, training and distribution. The groups used money from their successful businesses to buy more lamps.

B Alasdair Harris

Coastal communities in south-western Madagascar have lived by fishing for more than a thousand years. But when biologist Alasdair Harris visited the region, he found them struggling to sustain themselves because population increases had diminished local fish stocks. Unsurprisingly, people had mixed feelings when he suggested closing one of the local fishing grounds, but agreed to a three-month trial. When it was re-opened, they caught a staggering 1,200 kg of octopus in one day and the community could see the benefit of looking after their resources. Others soon took up the model and the country now boasts hundreds of marine areas, monitored and protected by local people. Organisations in neighbouring countries have begun to replicate the model, as recognition grows for the importance of locally initiated conservation. 'We need a radically new approach,' Alasdair says, 'that's why we do this work.'

C Nam Nguyen

Although much of Vietnam's population lives in rural areas, its two major cities are increasingly affected by traffic and pollution. Ride-sharing was a relatively new concept when Nam Nguyen founded his Hanoi-based ride-sharing website. Initially, he intended to make a free network where people could share vehicles and contribute to protecting the environment. 'I tried to learn the model from European schemes, but they didn't really work here. Private vehicles are a source of pride for many city dwellers, who rely on them to visit their families in the provinces. They wouldn't give them up easily.' He realised he'd have to form a business plan to help finance and promote the idea. So, Nam designed a taxi-sharing service whose profits could support the ride-sharing enterprise he had initially imagined. 'The taxi service has become our main revenue stream. It allows the ride-sharing network to continue to grow.'

D Bernice Dapaah

About to graduate with a business administration degree but facing a tough job market in Ghana, Bernice Dapaah joined forces with some engineering students to create an innovative product from bamboo, an abundant crop in Ghana. They make strong, lightweight and durable bikes out of bamboo, using an ever-growing team of young people specially trained for the role. The project has serious green credentials, too: not only are the bikes an affordable, environmentally sound alternative to cars, but bamboo is fast-growing, produces up to 35% more oxygen than other trees and helps to prevent soil erosion, a significant cause of concern for farmers. It's an idea so brilliant the team went on to win ten international awards. The initiative had soon sold over a thousand bikes, including exports, allowing new workshops to be set up. The idea is that each employee, once trained, can train and employ five others and bikes can be produced on a small scale all over Ghana.

WRITING (1 hour 20 minutes)

Part 1

You **must** answer this question. Write your answer in **140–190** words in an appropriate style **on the separate answer sheet**.

---

1 In your English class you have been talking about money for sports people. Now, your English teacher has asked you to write an essay.

Write your essay using **all** the notes and giving reasons for your point of view.

'Famous sports people are paid too much money.' Do you agree?

Notes

Write about:

1. the entertainment they provide
2. how hard they work
3. .... (your own idea)

Part 2

Write an answer to **one** of the questions **2–4** in this part. Write your answer in **140–190** words in an appropriate style **on the separate answer sheet**. Put the question number in the box at the top of the answer sheet.

---

2 In your English class you have been discussing why parks and green spaces are important for people living in towns and cities. Now your English teacher has asked you to write a report.

In your report, you should:

- describe the parks and green spaces in your area
- recommend ways of improving these green spaces
- say why these improvements would have a positive effect on people's lives.

Write your **report**.

3 You see this advertisement in the online magazine *Global Food*:

> **Wanted: Restaurant reviewer**
>
> We are looking for someone to write reviews of restaurants in your area. You should:
>
> - be able to take photographs to go with your reviews
> - be interested in different types of food
> - have a good level of English.
>
> Write to the magazine editor, Phil Simms, explaining why you are suitable for the job.

Write your **letter of application**.

4 You see this notice in an English-language magazine:

> *Articles wanted*
>
> **Technology**
>
> Which piece of technology would our lives be better without? Why?
>
> The best articles will be printed next month.

Write your **article**.

LISTENING (approximately 40 minutes)

Part 1

You will hear people talking in eight different situations.

For questions **1–8**, choose the best answer (**A**, **B** or **C**).

---

1 You hear a woman talking on the radio about an actor.

What does the woman say about him?

A His acting has improved over the years.

B The media often criticise him unfairly.

C He gets fewer film roles than he deserves.

2 You hear a hairstylist talking about her career.

She prefers working in the TV industry because she

A feels that her contribution is valued.

B is able to express her opinions freely.

C thrives on the creative challenge the work presents.

3 You hear a comedian called Geoff Knight talking on the radio about his profession.

What does Geoff like his act to contain?

A stories that give people a surprise

B things that everybody can relate to

C material that nobody has used before

4 You hear a conversation between a customer and a coffee shop employee.

What is the employee doing?

A waiting for a colleague's help

B excusing a colleague's inefficiency

C criticising a colleague's attitude

5 You hear a man telling a friend about an art exhibition.

What does he say about it?

A It was well attended.

B The lighting was effective.

C The catalogue was worth buying.

6 You overhear a man ringing a sports shop.

Why is he calling?

A to report an incident in the shop

B to make a special order

C to follow up an earlier query

7 You hear a man telling a friend about his work.

How does the man feel about his work?

A resentment of his colleague's success

B regret at the changes that have taken place

C frustration at his lack of progress

8 You hear two people talking about a country walk they're doing.

What do they agree about?

A It's much too long to complete.

B The path is very difficult to follow.

C They've chosen the wrong day to do it.

Part 2

You will hear a presentation given by a university student called Megan Rowlings about a forest survival course she went on in Australia. For questions **9–18**, complete the sentences with a word or short phrase.

Survival in the forest

It was Megan's **(9)** .... who told her about the survival course.

Megan particularly appreciated the course leader John's use of **(10)** .... at stressful moments.

Megan said the assistant's knowledge of **(11)** .... was very useful during the course.

Megan was worried that her **(12)** .... would be a problem in doing some of the tasks.

John emphasised that when it comes to safety, **(13)** .... is the most dangerous reaction.

Megan's teammates were grateful for the **(14)** .... which she'd brought with her.

Megan learned how to make a **(15)** .... from the material found in the forest.

Megan and her group were told they should only use water from the **(16)** .... for drinking.

Megan found that making a **(17)** .... was hard for her.

Megan was surprised to find that the skill of **(18)** .... benefited her.

Part 3

You will hear five short extracts in which people talk about a problem they had in their first few weeks in a new job. For questions **19–23**, choose what problem (**A–H**) each speaker says they had. Use the letters only once. There are three extra letters which you do not need to use.

A I made an embarrassing comment.

B I didn't get on with my colleagues.

C I took on too much work.

D I didn't get enough support.

E I found the work too challenging.

F I was over-confident.

G I wasn't very punctual.

H I was treated unreasonably.

Speaker 1		**19**
Speaker 2		**20**
Speaker 3		**21**
Speaker 4		**22**
Speaker 5		**23**

Part 4

You will hear an interview with an international concert pianist called Karen Hong. For questions **24–30**, choose the best answer (**A**, **B** or **C**).

---

24 Why does Karen keep practising pieces of music she knows well?

A to keep her confidence levels high

B to warm up before playing difficult new pieces

C to make small improvements to her performance of them

25 What does Karen say about her mother?

A She still tries to have an influence over Karen.

B She shows her emotions much more than Karen's father.

C She could have been a competent pianist herself.

26 Karen says that after winning a big competition, she began

A to lose interest in music.

B to take offence easily.

C to doubt her talent.

27 Karen's decision to take a break from performing allowed her to

A spend a lot of time on her own.

B regain full physical health.

C put a new management team in place.

28 When she was performing on television regularly, Karen enjoyed the idea that

A she was bringing people from different countries closer together.

B she was improving people's mood and energy levels.

C she was taking classical music to new places and people.

29 What does Karen say about pop music?

A It is suitable for people of all ages.

B It makes little impression on her.

C It affects teenagers' behaviour in different ways.

30 Karen believes that when dealing with young children who play music

A praise should only be given where it is justified.

B pushing them too hard will demotivate them.

C it's a mistake to make them nervous about the end result.

SPEAKING (14 minutes)

You take the Speaking test with another candidate (possibly two candidates), referred to here as your partner. There are two examiners. One will speak to you and your partner and the other will be listening. Both examiners will award marks.

Part 1 (2 minutes)

The examiner asks you and your partner questions about yourselves. You may be asked about things like 'your home town', 'your interests', 'your career plans', etc.

Part 2 (a one-minute 'long turn' for each candidate, plus a 30-second response from the second candidate)

The examiner gives you two photographs and asks you to talk about them for one minute. The examiner then asks your partner a question about your photographs and your partner responds briefly.

Then the examiner gives your partner two different photographs. Your partner talks about these photographs for one minute. This time the examiner asks you a question about your partner's photographs and you respond briefly.

Part 3 (4 minutes)

The examiner asks you and your partner to talk together. They give you a task to look at so you can think about and discuss an idea, giving reasons for your opinion. For example, you may be asked to think about some changes in the world, or about spending free time with your family. After you have discussed the task for about two minutes with your partner, the examiner will ask you a follow-up question, which you should discuss for a further minute.

Part 4 (4 minutes)

The examiner asks some further questions, which leads to a more general discussion of what you have talked about in Part 3. You may comment on your partner's answers if you wish.

Test 2

READING AND USE OF ENGLISH (1 hour 15 minutes)

Part 1

For questions **1–8**, read the text below and decide which answer (**A**, **B**, **C** or **D**) best fits each gap. There is an example at the beginning (**0**).

Mark your answers on the **separate answer sheet**.

Example:

0 **A** ways **B** methods **C** manners **D** types

0	A	B	C	D
	▬	▭	▭	▭

Tea bags

Over the centuries, tea has been made in many different **(0)** .... across the world. In the USA, until a little over a hundred years ago, dried tea was always sold and consumed as loose leaves. To make a drink, boiling water was poured over the tea leaves and **(1)** .... to stand while the water **(2)** .... the flavour of the leaves.

In 1908, Thomas Sullivan, a New York tea salesman, had the **(3)** .... idea of putting tea leaves in small silk bags to **(4)** .... as samples to potential customers. Sullivan **(5)** .... the tea to be removed from the bags before making a drink in the conventional manner. However, for the sake of **(6)** .... , his customers **(7)** .... up with the revolutionary practice of dipping the silk bag, contents and all, into boiling water. Cheap paper bags were introduced in the 1930s, completing the design of the modern tea bag. Today billions of **(8)** .... paper bags of tea are sold annually worldwide.

1	**A**	set	**B**	kept	**C**	left	**D**	saved
2	**A**	immersed	**B**	soaked	**C**	filled	**D**	absorbed
3	**A**	sharp	**B**	bright	**C**	light	**D**	keen
4	**A**	put in	**B**	give up	**C**	hand out	**D**	make over
5	**A**	intended	**B**	determined	**C**	designed	**D**	established
6	**A**	satisfaction	**B**	benefit	**C**	convenience	**D**	opportunity
7	**A**	thought	**B**	came	**C**	started	**D**	made
8	**A**	distinct	**B**	particular	**C**	specific	**D**	individual

Part 2

For questions **9–16**, read the text below and think of the word which best fits each gap. Use only **one** word in each gap. There is an example at the beginning (**0**).

Write your answers **IN CAPITAL LETTERS on the separate answer sheet**.

Example: | 0 | A R E |

Kangaroos

Kangaroos **(0)** .... found in the wild only in Australia and its surrounding islands. There are several species of kangaroo but the best known are the large red, grey and antilopine kangaroos. They all have large feet and extremely strong back legs as **(9)** .... as a long tail, and can grow up to 1.6 metres tall. They tend to jump rather **(10)** .... walk because their large feet make walking difficult.

The one fact that almost **(11)** .... knows about kangaroos is that young kangaroos, joeys, live in a kind of pocket at the front of their mother's body. Although they may come **(12)** .... of the pocket to play or explore, the pocket is **(13)** .... they live for many months after their birth.

Kangaroos feed on grasses, leaves, flowers and moss. They live in groups known **(14)** .... mobs and protect one **(15)** .... from danger. They present **(16)** .... serious threat to human beings because they rarely attack people, and only if provoked.

Part 3

For questions **17–24**, read the text below. Use the word given in capitals at the end of some of the lines to form a word that fits in the gap **in the same line**. There is an example at the beginning (**0**).

Write your answers **IN CAPITAL LETTERS on the separate answer sheet**.

Example: | 0 | V | A | R | I | E | T | Y |

Bicycle racing

There is a wide **(0)** .... of different types of bicycle racing. A race may be an event held indoors over a relatively short distance, or alternatively it can be outdoors and much longer, involving hundreds of kilometres over a number of days. As the **(17)** .... of bicycle	**VARY** / **POPULAR**

There is a wide **(0)** .... of different types of bicycle racing. A race **VARY**
may be an event held indoors over a relatively short distance, or
alternatively it can be outdoors and much longer, involving hundreds
of kilometres over a number of days. As the **(17)** .... of bicycle **POPULAR**
racing has grown worldwide, attention has focussed increasingly
on the **(18)** .... study of the sport and its many physical and **SCIENCE**
psychological **(19)** .... There seems to be agreement among **REQUIRE**
sports experts that competitive cycling, more than almost any other
sport, places **(20)** .... demands on the whole human body. **EXCEPT**

Successful participants in many sports can be a bit **(21)** .... or **FIT**
slightly overweight but nevertheless have sufficient **(22)** .... to **ABLE**
compensate for that. That is not true for serious cyclists who aim to
do well in competitions. They must show extraordinary dedication
to the sport. Many seem to have an **(23)** .... with it and an **OBSESS**
(24) .... of the hours and hours of practice necessary to achieve **ACCEPT**
success.

Part 4

For questions **25–30**, complete the second sentence so that it has a similar meaning to the first sentence, using the word given. **Do not change the word given**. You must use between **two** and **five** words, including the word given. Here is an example (**0**).

Example:

0 A very friendly taxi driver drove us into town.

DRIVEN

We .... a very friendly taxi driver.

The gap can be filled by the words 'were driven into town by', so you write:

Example:	**0**	*WERE DRIVEN INTO TOWN BY*

Write **only** the missing words **IN CAPITAL LETTERS on the separate answer sheet.**

---

25 John had never been in that part of the country before.

FIRST

It .... that John had ever been in that part of the country.

26 I wish I could play the guitar, but I can't.

ABLE

I would .... play the guitar, but I can't.

27 The public swimming pool didn't use to be so crowded.

THAN

The public swimming pool is .... to be.

28 Nobody knows for certain the depth of the water in the middle of the lake.

DEEP

Nobody knows for certain .... in the middle of the lake.

29 Although the room became quite noisy, the singer continued singing.

EVEN

The singer carried .... the room became quite noisy.

30 I have never seen an elephant as large as the one in the film.

SUCH

I haven't .... elephant as the one in the film.

Part 5

You are going to read an article about a man who makes guitars. For questions **31–36**, choose the answer (**A**, **B**, **C** or **D**) which you think fits best according to the text.

Mark your answers **on the separate answer sheet**.

The guitar maker

Jonny Kinkead, one of the best known makers of hand-crafted acoustic guitars in the UK, talks about his career.

As a boy, when Jonny Kinkead wasn't making things using the tools in his dad's garage, he was messing about with a guitar. And the two preoccupations have been his living for the past four decades: building steel-string, acoustic guitars by hand. 'The guitar still holds me in thrall,' he says. 'Making a sound out of planks of wood – it's amazing what you can do. By using different combinations of timber, for example, you get a different sound, and that is what musicians are interested in – a sound that can do what they want it to do.'

Jonny learned to play his brother's guitar when he was eleven. Then, when he was sixteen, he wanted to learn the bass guitar. 'Some people would have got a holiday job and saved up and bought one,' he says. 'But I was of a mindset that if you wanted something, you made it.'

Although the bass was the first instrument Jonny built from scratch, he and his brothers had long been doing essentially the same thing with other items. 'I made model boats and aeroplanes as a child, so I was familiar with that process. My father had taught me and my brothers how to use tools, and we had free rein in the garage.' Jonny had also been customising and repairing instruments for his mates.

Jonny's bass guitar turned out well, but the idea of a career building guitars had yet to cross his mind. 'My ambition in those days was to be a sculptor,' he says. His interests evolved further and on finishing school, he chose to study architecture at university. Halfway through the course, however, he dropped out, but he left with a clearer idea of what he wanted to do and started to think seriously about guitar making. 'I was still interested in painting and sculpture but I realised that when you are building guitars you're actually sculpting sound.' In addition he explains, 'I thought this might be more reliable than being an artist as it's craft-based.'

Ever since then, Jonny has made guitars for a living. For the first ten years, he supplemented his income by cleaning windows part-time. The first guitars he sold only went for the cost of the materials, but as he developed a reputation as one of the best guitar-makers around, he was able to charge a little more. But even now, almost forty years later, Jonny describes what he does as 'still scratching a living'. He admits he can never actually turn out more than ten guitars a year, which inevitably restricts his earnings.

In the early years, the key thing was to make the effort to get himself known. He would go to music festivals most weekends if he could and get musicians to try out his guitars and talk about him to their friends. He also had to learn how to price his instruments – when it came up in conversations with musicians, he hadn't got an answer because focusing on such things didn't come naturally to him.

Jonny believes developing a career is more straightforward for today's new guitar-makers in the UK. 'When I started it was hard because people thought that the guitars I was making were only made in America and that people in the UK didn't know how to make them. Now there is a culture of hand-making guitars that has grown up over the past 40 years in the UK. It is easier now for them,' he says. You may be able to learn valuable techniques in the classroom, Jonny concludes, but there is no substitute for trial and error, 'Make 100 guitars and you learn a lot.'

31 Why did Jonny choose to make a bass guitar for himself when he was a teenager?

A He regarded it as the natural thing to do.
B He saw it as good practice for making other guitars.
C He feared that he would never be able to buy one.
D He thought he could ensure it was in the style he wanted.

32 What does 'that process' in line 25 refer to?

A creating something from nothing
B working with his brothers
C doing things for friends
D getting tools ready

33 What does Jonny say about the architecture course he attended?

A It gave him the opportunity to explore different types of art.
B It provided him with ideas for guitar design.
C It enabled him to decide on a career path.
D It helped him become more independent.

34 What does Jonny suggest is the main reason for his low income?

A the cost of the materials he makes guitars with
B the small number of guitars that he produces
C the limited demand for hand-made guitars
D the competition between guitar-makers

35 What does Jonny say he found hard in his early years as a guitar-maker?

A deciding how much to charge for his guitars
B working out how to advertise his services
C building up relationships with musicians
D finding the time to visit music festivals

36 What does Jonny think has changed for guitar-makers in the UK?

A The training they receive is of a higher standard.
B A wider range of tools and equipment is available.
C Attitudes towards what makes a good guitar have moved on.
D Work methods have been introduced from America.

Part 6

You are going to read a newspaper article about the filming of a television documentary about icebergs. Six sentences have been removed from the article. Choose from the sentences **A–G** the one which fits each gap (**37–42**). There is one extra sentence which you do not need to use.

Mark your answers **on the separate answer sheet.**

Icebergs

There's more to icebergs than meets the eye – as I discovered filming on one of these gigantic Arctic fortresses as it slowly melted.

Imagine a solid sheet of frozen water 3 km across and 100 m thick. Imagine it floating quietly in dark ocean waters, somewhere between Canada and Greenland. Imagine the near-silent desolation of the inhospitable Arctic environment around it, getting harsher as winter approaches. **37** Imagine this forbidding, serene, massive place. But it really exists. This iceberg right now is floating in peace as we all go about our busy, bustling lives.

Back in the summer, things were different. This iceberg was a dynamic battleground, floodlit by 24-hour daylight. Once an iceberg is released from its parent glacier, its time is very limited. **38** Then mini-bergs break off the weakened front. Some of these events we witnessed were sudden, loud and violent. We had come to spectate on this oceanic siege, and to learn its rules.

The ice edge towered over us, vertical, angular and utterly spectacular. We steamed around the berg until we found lower cliffs, and suddenly the icescape behind was revealed. Gentle mounds are separated by valleys. **39** An iceberg makes its own fog, so we could only see a little way into the centre, peering hopefully over the top of the cliffs.

Curious polar bears peered back. We had thought we would be lucky to see one or two, but the iceberg turned out to have a healthy population of these huge carnivores. **40** They must wait for the sea ice to come back so that they can hunt. So they were snoozing away, not at all bothered that their chosen holiday home was moving, tilting, melting, breaking up and giving a TV production team and some scientists severe logistical headaches.

That's how I remember the iceberg, and that's the side of it you'll see if you watch the programmes. But since then things have changed. We left a GPS tracker as a passenger, so we know that the iceberg has travelled 60 miles, and is now about 30 miles south of where it was in August. Only 65% of it is left. The iceberg only gets 7 hours and 40 minutes of daylight now, and soon the darkness will swallow it up completely. **41** Winter is beginning, and with it returns a period of stability.

Sea ice is advancing towards the berg from the north. This is the other type of ice at the poles, formed when the sea surface itself freezes. In an average year, the sea ice would already have reached our iceberg. But this year, there was less summer sea ice in the Arctic than any other year on record, so it is taking longer for the great freeze to reach it. The sea ice is still crawling south. **42** Then the iceberg will be frozen in place. Darkness and silence will rule. The bears will be able to walk out on to the sea ice and hunt again.

A These lead down to waterfalls of meltwater cascading into the ocean.

B But it will lose the battle in the end and the last piece of solid ice will melt.

C When it touches the cliffs that I saw, it will connect our iceberg to all the other ice in the Arctic.

D The ice fights a losing battle along its edges, as warm ocean water eats into it.

E The only sound comes from water lapping against the ice, and a lone seal swimming nearby.

F The Arctic summer can, however, be a very hard time for them.

G The supply of energy from the sun is so weak, the battle is over for this year.

Part 7

You are going to read an article about a new exercise craze called *Zuu* and its inventor Nathan Helberg. For questions **43–52**, choose from sections (**A–E**). The sections may be chosen more than once.

Mark your answers **on the separate answer sheet**.

In which section does the writer

comment on how little rest she seems to be given after one exercise?	**43**	
become aware of the limitations of her usual fitness routine?	**44**	
say she hopes that the next exercise is not so demanding?	**45**	
mention a deal she did with Nathan that benefited them both?	**46**	
imply that a conventional keep-fit method is less natural than *Zuu*?	**47**	
compare the movements of *Zuu* with those of earlier humans?	**48**	
explain that she has chosen just one of the exercises to perform regularly?	**49**	
say how slow and awkward she feels doing a particular exercise?	**50**	
give examples of situations where lack of activity affects people's bodies?	**51**	
cast doubt on one of Nathan's ideas?	**52**	

Exercise like an animal

Journalist Annabel Venning tries a new exercise craze

A ____________________

Our sedentary lifestyles mean that most of us aren't using our muscles properly. As small children we squat, crawl and leap around freely, but the older we get the more restricted our movements become and many of our muscles get little action as we sit at desks or in cars. Occasionally we hit the gym, where we use machines to work on specific muscles rather than the whole body. Now a new form of fitness, an intense workout based on simple animal movements such as crawling, is taking off. Its Australian founder, Nathan Helberg, has been using it with the military, police forces, schoolchildren and even prisoners. He took his inspiration from martial arts, break-dancing, the animal world and the dance movements of indigenous people, and developed *Zuu*.

B ____________________

There are around 100 animal movements – although beginners start with 25 – that work muscles, joints and ligaments as well as improving heart and lung fitness. *Zuu* needs no equipment and little space. The idea is to train your body to do the kinds of activities that our ancestors had to do in daily life. It's quick, it tops up your strength and it's not aiming to give you big muscles. In exchange for the publicity from my article, Nathan offers me a master class, alongside two of his trainers, a privilege that would otherwise be beyond my financial means! I am daunted by the prospect of doing things I haven't done since my pre-school years.

C ____________________

We do each movement for 30 seconds (for my benefit – as you get fitter, you keep on for 45 seconds). We start with a frog squat: legs wide, knees bent, elbows locked inside knees. It's a little undignified, but fine at first. Then as the seconds go by, the fronts of my thighs start to burn and it's all I can do not to collapse. After the 30 seconds we dash back across the room to our starting point with barely a moment to catch our breath. Nathan assures me the frog squat is particularly good for the lower backs of office workers, and recommends that they should take a break and perform the movement for four minutes a day. Somehow I can't see this working!

D ____________________

Then it's on to a bear crawl, on hands and feet. While Nathan and others shoot across the room, I lumber along like an ancient grizzly bear. Then we do it again – backwards. I seem to be clumsy, but it does get slightly easier as I go on. This movement evidently uses every joint in the body, strengthening things like ligaments and tendons, while at the same time raising heart rate as effectively as running. Perhaps being a snake will be easier. But there's no lying flat on our stomachs. Instead we have to raise our bodies 2 cm off the floor, rocking our weight back and forth from hands to toes. It's a bit of an effort to keep going for the full minute.

E ____________________

By the end I'm shaking with exhaustion. Despite my initial reservations, by the end of my session, I have started to enjoy myself. Mind you, it's hard not to laugh when you're imitating a bear on rewind! I thought I was in reasonably good shape – I run 5 km three times a week – but after this I realise how little I push myself normally. Nathan has promised that I could increase my upper body strength by 30% in just six weeks by doing classes. I have compromised and do bear crawls around my garden at home during work breaks, much to the amazement of my dog!

WRITING (1 hour 20 minutes)

Part 1

You **must** answer this question. Write your answer in **140–190** words in an appropriate style **on the separate answer sheet**.

---

1 In your English class you have been talking about self-employment. Now, your English teacher has asked you to write an essay.

Write your essay using **all** the notes and giving reasons for your point of view.

Is it better to be self-employed or to work for somebody else?

Notes

Write about:

1. being independent

2. job security

3. .... (your own idea)

Part 2

Write an answer to **one** of the questions **2–4** in this part. Write your answer in **140–190** words in an appropriate style **on the separate answer sheet**. Put the question number in the box at the top of the answer sheet.

---

2 You have seen this notice in an online holiday magazine:

> *Reviews wanted*
>
> **Sports Holidays**
>
> We're looking for reviews of organised holidays where people can practise sports.
>
> Write a review of the holiday, including information about the place, the sports, and how well organised the holiday was.

Write your **review**.

3 You see this notice in an English-language magazine:

> *Articles wanted*
>
> **Being famous for something**
>
> If you could be famous for something, what would you like to be famous for? Why?
>
> The best articles will be printed next month.

Write your **article**.

4 You receive this email from your English-speaking friend, Nico:

> **Subject: Where to study?**
>
> Hi
> I'm going to university next year. I can either go to the university in my home town and live at home, or study in another area and live away from home.
> What do you think I should do?
> Write soon
> Nico

Write your **email**.

LISTENING (approximately 40 minutes)

Part 1

You will hear people talking in eight different situations.

For questions **1–8**, choose the best answer (**A**, **B** or **C**).

---

1 You hear a man talking about collecting old coins.

What pleases him most about his hobby?

A the satisfaction of aiming for a complete collection

B the idea that someone has used the coins in the past

C the thrill of searching for unusual coins for his collection

2 You hear a woman talking about playing the piano.

What does she say about learning to play the piano?

A It's important to find the right teacher.

B Everyone can play well if they try.

C It requires more discipline than other instruments.

3 You overhear a man and a woman talking in an art gallery about a boy's paintings.

What do they agree about the paintings?

A They show remarkable artistic maturity.

B The gallery is asking too much money for them.

C They probably weren't painted by the boy.

4 You hear two students talking about a university chemistry lecturer.

What do they agree about the lecturer?

A She is good at explaining difficult concepts in lectures.

B She is tolerant towards students who hand work in late.

C She manages to make students feel enthusiastic about her subject.

5 You hear a woman talking to a work colleague about moving abroad for a new job.

What does the woman feel disappointed about?

A the inflexible attitude to the start date

B the lack of job security involved

C the relatively low status of the work

6 You hear two friends talking about a job interview.

How does the woman feel now?

A surprised that the interview went well

B pleased to have impressed the interviewers

C relieved that she wasn't asked any difficult questions

7 You hear part of a radio programme

What is the woman talking about?

A an environment group

B a nature course for school children

C a new walking route in the countryside

8 You hear a woman talking to her brother about his hair.

What is she doing?

A admitting she cut his hair badly

B teasing him about his haircut

C suggesting he grow his hair longer

Part 2

You will hear a man called David Briggs giving a talk about his work as a volunteer on a turtle conservation programme in Western Australia. For questions **9–18**, complete the sentences with a word or short phrase.

Working on a turtle conservation programme

David first found out about the turtle programme from his **(9)** ....

David chose to work at the **(10)** .... site because its location was more convenient.

David thinks his interest in **(11)** .... helped him to get a place on the programme.

David was surprised to find that the ability to **(12)** .... wasn't considered necessary.

Apart from the cost of **(13)** .... everything essential was provided by the organisers.

David's shifts took place during the **(14)** .... when the turtles could be checked on the beach.

David felt it was particularly important to be **(15)** .... when handling the turtles.

Unlike his fellow volunteers, David found the **(16)** .... didn't bother him.

David said that tiredness could lead to a loss of **(17)** .... among the volunteers when they were collecting data.

David uses the name **(18)** .... to refer to the most experienced volunteers.

Part 3

You will hear five short extracts in which writers give advice about writing comedy scripts for television. For questions **19–23**, choose which piece of advice (**A–H**) each speaker gives. Use the letters only once. There are three extra letters which you do not need to use.

A Write about people who amuse you.

B Team up with another writer.

C Develop your characters well.

D Rewrite your whole script several times.

E Study comedy you like.

F Listen to what other people say about your work.

G Find your own way as a writer.

H Let the audience in on the joke quickly.

Speaker 1		**19**
Speaker 2		**20**
Speaker 3		**21**
Speaker 4		**22**
Speaker 5		**23**

Part 4

You will hear an interview with a woman called Maya Gardi, whose daily life and business are based on waste-free principles. For questions **24–30**, choose the best answer (**A**, **B** or **C**).

---

24 What did Maya find most difficult when she started shopping in a waste-free way?

A having to take more time over it

B having to avoid things in plastic containers

C having to remember to take her own bags

25 Maya decided to adopt a completely waste-free lifestyle when she

A saw an article online about plastic rubbish.

B noticed the bins outside her block of flats.

C visited her local waste facitilty.

26 How did Maya's parents react to her decision to live waste-free?

A They were worried that she would regret it.

B They did not believe that she really meant it.

C They did not think that she was likely to succeed.

27 How have Maya's cooking and eating habits changed?

A She uses leftover food creatively.

B She cooks more often for her friends.

C She has developed her own cooking skills.

28 What does Maya say about socialising?

A She sometimes has to forget her principles.

B She doesn't worry about what people think of her.

C She carefully chooses which events she attends.

29 What does Maya say about her new business?

A She has an advantage when it comes to marketing.

B Sales are increasing faster than expected.

C She is expanding into a related sector.

30 How did Maya feel about the radio work she did recently?

A nervous about taking part at the last minute

B pleased to have the chance to explain her views

C surprised that she was asked by a reporter

SPEAKING (14 minutes)

You take the Speaking test with another candidate (possibly two candidates), referred to here as your partner. There are two examiners. One will speak to you and your partner and the other will be listening. Both examiners will award marks.

Part 1 (2 minutes)

The examiner asks you and your partner questions about yourselves. You may be asked about things like 'your home town', 'your interests', 'your career plans', etc.

Part 2 (a one-minute 'long turn' for each candidate, plus a 30-second response from the second candidate)

The examiner gives you two photographs and asks you to talk about them for one minute. The examiner then asks your partner a question about your photographs and your partner responds briefly.

Then the examiner gives your partner two different photographs. Your partner talks about these photographs for one minute. This time the examiner asks you a question about your partner's photographs and you respond briefly.

Part 3 (4 minutes)

The examiner asks you and your partner to talk together. They give you a task to look at so you can think about and discuss an idea, giving reasons for your opinion. For example, you may be asked to think about some changes in the world, or about spending free time with your family. After you have discussed the task for about two minutes with your partner, the examiner will ask you a follow-up question, which you should discuss for a further minute.

Part 4 (4 minutes)

The examiner asks some further questions, which leads to a more general discussion of what you have talked about in Part 3. You may comment on your partner's answers if you wish.

Test 3

READING AND USE OF ENGLISH (1 hour 15 minutes)

Part 1

For questions **1–8**, read the text below and decide which answer (**A**, **B**, **C** or **D**) best fits each gap. There is an example at the beginning (**0**).

Mark your answers **on the separate answer sheet**.

Example:

0 **A** devised **B** invented **C** thought **D** constructed

0	A	B	C	D
	▭	▬	▭	▭

Imaginary friends in early childhood

Many children have an imaginary friend – that is a friend they have **(0)** .... It was once thought that only children who had difficulty in **(1)** .... relationships with others had imaginary friends. In fact, having an imaginary friend is probably a common **(2)** .... of a normal childhood as many children with lots of real friends also have an imaginary friend. The imaginary friend may help some children **(3)** .... with emotional difficulties, but for many, having an imaginary friend is just fun.

Most children, it appears, realise that their imaginary friend is not real. If people **(4)** .... asking about an imaginary friend, children often say, 'You know, my friend isn't real – I **(5)** .... him up.'

There is no firm evidence to say that having an imaginary friend **(6)** .... us anything about what a child will be like in the future. One **(7)** .... of research, though, has **(8)** .... that adults who once had imaginary friends may be more creative than those who did not.

1	**A** forming	**B** creating	**C** gaining	**D** producing
2	**A** state	**B** aspect	**C** situation	**D** point
3	**A** handle	**B** accept	**C** support	**D** cope
4	**A** keep	**B** persist	**C** maintain	**D** stay
5	**A** got	**B** put	**C** made	**D** set
6	**A** reveals	**B** informs	**C** tells	**D** advises
7	**A** item	**B** section	**C** unit	**D** piece
8	**A** suggested	**B** displayed	**C** presented	**D** notified

Part 2

For questions **9–16**, read the text below and think of the word which best fits each gap. Use only **one** word in each gap. There is an example at the beginning (**0**).

Write your answers **IN CAPITAL LETTERS on the separate answer sheet.**

Example:	0	B	E	E	N

Collecting stamps

Ever since postage stamps were first issued, people have **(0)** .... collecting them. At **(9)** .... this was regarded as just a hobby for children. Many people, though, continue collecting stamps throughout the whole of **(10)** .... lives. Although stamp collecting is no **(11)** .... as widespread as it once was, it remains **(12)** .... of the most popular hobbies.

The collections people make vary. Some want to obtain every stamp ever issued by a particular country. Others, though, are more interested in the pictures on stamps and collect as **(13)** .... stamps as possible which have, for example, a picture of a bird or maybe of an aeroplane.

It is **(14)** .... doubt very satisfying for a collector to feel such a collection is complete. However, in many cases this never happens **(15)** .... new stamps are being issued **(16)** .... the time. This may seem frustrating but it means that people can carry on collecting for as long as their interest lasts.

Part 3

For questions **17–24**, read the text below. Use the word given in capitals at the end of some of the lines to form a word that fits in the gap **in the same line**. There is an example at the beginning (**0**).

Write your answers **IN CAPITAL LETTERS on the separate answer sheet**.

Example: | 0 | D | A | N | G | E | R | O | U | S |

The transcontinental railway

Before 1869 the journey from the east coast to the west coast of	
the United States took between four and six months, travelling	
through difficult and **(0)** .... country by wagon. With the west	**DANGER**
coast becoming increasingly wealthy it was obvious that a better	
route was needed. In the 1850s **(17)** .... began about building a	**DISCUSS**
transcontinental railway line linking the west with the east.	
Although there was much **(18)** .... about the best route, eventually	**AGREEMENT**
it was decided to build a line. It ran 3,069 kilometres in **(19)**	**LONG**
from Sacramento in the west to a point where it would join **(20)**	**EXIST**
lines giving access to the east coast.	
Once the line became operational in 1869, the journey could be	
completed in less than a week. In **(21)** .... with the six hours that a	**COMPARE**
(22) .... from New York to San Francisco takes nowadays, this may	**FLY**
not seem particularly **(23)** ...., but building the transcontinental	**IMPRESS**
railway was a great technological **(24)** .... which helped to bring	**ACHIEVE**
unity to the country.	

Part 4

For questions **25–30**, complete the second sentence so that it has a similar meaning to the first sentence, using the word given. **Do not change the word given**. You must use between **two** and **five** words, including the word given. Here is an example (**0**).

Example:

0 A very friendly taxi driver drove us into town.

DRIVEN

We .... a very friendly taxi driver.

The gap can be filled by the words 'were driven into town by', so you write:

Example:	**0**	*WERE DRIVEN INTO TOWN BY*

Write **only** the missing words **IN CAPITAL LETTERS on the separate answer sheet.**

---

25 There was nobody with my brother when the accident happened.

OWN

My brother .... when the accident happened.

26 I read only the first three chapters of the book because it was so boring.

GAVE

I .... the book after the first three chapters because it was so boring.

27 I found it difficult to get on with my work because it was so hot.

MADE

The heat .... me to get on with my work.

28 Sigmund accidentally left the door unlocked over the weekend.

MEAN

Sigmund .... the door unlocked over the weekend.

29 Mr Bateman was wrong to say that John had lost my keys.

SHOULD

Mr Bateman .... that John had lost my keys.

30 The opening of the new restaurant has been postponed for two weeks.

BE

It .... the new restaurant opens.

Part 5

You are going to read an article about a race between two famous brothers. For questions **31–36**, choose the answer (**A**, **B**, **C** or **D**) which you think fits best according to the text.

Mark your answers **on the separate answer sheet**.

An unusual race

To raise money for charity, a newspaper and a TV company challenged brothers Jonny and Alistair Brownlee, champion triathletes, to take part in a unique race that would set man against car, and brother against brother. In the wild and mountainous Yorkshire Dales of northern England, Jonny and younger brother Alistair would race to the same point, Jonny in a car on roads, Alistair across country on a mountain bike.

'I'm looking forward to it,' Jonny said, as the brothers took their places on the start line. 'I've never done anything like this before: it's exciting! These roads have beautiful views – and also it's very cold at the moment, so I'll be able to sit in the car and stay nice and warm.' Alistair was similarly eager – though in contrast to Jonny's jeans and sweatshirt, he was decked out in full winter cycling gear. Not that the cold was denting his confidence. 'To be honest,' he said, 'I've seen his driving before, so I'm not sure he's even going to make it. I might just stop for a cup of tea halfway up.'

The race started at the beautiful Semerwater lake in Wensleydale and was to finish at Yorkshire's highest road, Fleet Moss, some 350 metres up. No problem for the car, perhaps – but with Alistair's first couple of miles involving a 25 per cent incline, the younger Brownlee brother had his work cut out from the start. Barely time for a quick handshake and they were off. As Alistair sprinted away on his bike, heading for a track going straight up the hill and then across country to Fleet Moss, Jonny jumped in the car and was soon on the road. The next time the brothers would see each other would be at the finish line.

Jonny's early confidence took an immediate blow. Barely 15 seconds into the drive and he faced his first obstacle. Lumbering out of a field and into the road was a giant tractor. 'Welcome to Yorkshire,' he complained to the cameraman in the back of his car. 'If Alistair beats me, it's all down to this farmer!' Tense moments later, the tractor safely dealt with, Jonny was back in control.

Alistair, meanwhile, was struggling with the slope. Barely a couple of miles in and, as his brother relaxed, he was forced to dismount and carry his bike up the hill, past walls and over fences. Bemused sheep gazed, as the Olympic champion kept up a steady pace, at the bizarre sight of a man in a field with a bike on his shoulders. And then, finally, the summit was reached. Over the other side was open ground, and with the sun coming out and the land spread before him, a chance to show what he was made of. Head down, feet on the pedals, Alistair was picking up speed.

In the car, his brother faced another local obstacle. The villages in this part of Yorkshire have stood since well before the invention of the car – and the roads that link them were not exactly made for speed. Jonny attempted to negotiate another absurdly narrow corner. The car slowed to a crawl, then passed through a stream that had formed on the road.

Clear of the last village, the car was on a straight race to the finishing line. Neither brother knew how close the other was. As Jonny roared the engine and sped through the final straight to Fleet Moss, Alistair was flying across his last field and back onto the road himself – approaching the finish from the other side. Head down, legs pumping… and then a squeal of brakes as he reached the line. And then, finally, Alistair looked up. 'Is he here?' he asked the waiting crowd. 'No? Really?' The head went back, the arms up. 'Yes!' Minutes later, the car pulled up and Jonny stepped out. 'Well done,' Jonny said with disappointment. 'I'm gutted.'

31 The writer explains that before the race the brothers were alike in

A being dressed for difficult conditions.
B having plenty of enthusiasm for it.
C feeling anxious about the weather.
D believing in their own ability to win.

32 What is suggested about the start of the race?

A The brothers appeared very uncertain of the route.
B Alistair's training had been insufficient.
C Jonny had a noticeable advantage.
D The brothers tried to avoid eye contact with each other.

33 What is suggested about Alistair in the fifth paragraph?

A He objected to the situation he found himself in.
B He was relieved the hill was easier than expected.
C He welcomed an opportunity to prove his ability.
D He was distracted by the behaviour of some animals.

34 What does 'Bemused' mean in line 51?

A annoyed
B puzzled
C distressed
D disappointed

35 In the sixth paragraph, what do we learn about Jonny's progress?

A He had to briefly break the speed limit.
B He almost drove into some water.
C He had to get the car through a tight space.
D He nearly lost control of the car.

36 How did Alistair react when he reached the end of the race?

A He worried his brother had got lost.
B He celebrated by jumping off his bike.
C He congratulated his brother on his performance.
D He was uncertain who the winner was.

Part 6

You are going to read an article about a dam removal project. Six sentences have been removed from the article. Choose from the sentences **A–G** the one which fits each gap (**37–42**). There is one extra sentence which you do not need to use.

Mark your answers **on the separate answer sheet.**

Removing a dam to restore a river

Journalist Richard Lovett is taken to see how a river has come to life again after a dam has been removed.

Just outside the small town of Stabler in Washington, hydrologist Bengt Coffin surveys a mountain river he helped to revive. Today, the clear waters of Trout Creek run fast between banks covered in young alder trees. But just five years ago, an eight-metre-high concrete wall blocked the river at the site. This dam and the reservoir behind it had changed the river completely and made it difficult for fish such as the endangered steelhead trout to return to where they were born in order to breed. For one thing, the reservoir was full of sediment – mud, sand and gravel. It was Coffin who led the US Forest Service effort to remove the dam.

This is all part of a growing trend in the United States. An increasing number of dams are being removed, for financial and environmental reasons. **37** ____ Some schemes take a slow path, restoring river flow over months or years. Others use explosives and other engineering techniques to drain reservoirs within hours.

At Trout Creek, Coffin and his colleagues decided to take the cautious route when removing the ageing Hemlock Dam. **38** ____ The dam had been designed to include what is called a fish ladder, which allows fish and other animals to bypass the dam and swim upstream, but it was poorly built by modern standards and the number of fish using it had steadily declined.

A bigger concern was the reservoir, which had been steadily filling in with sediment. **39** ____ Coffin holds a hand above his knee to make the point. In the midsummer sun, temperatures in the water could reach 26°C; 'Too warm for steelhead,' he says.

Coffin and others worried that flooding the river with all that sediment would harm the steelhead further downstream. The solution was to divert the river into a big pipe and then hire a fleet of dumper trucks to carry away all the sediment. **40** ____ They then reinforced its banks with logs to stop them from eroding.

All those efforts seem to have worked. Just seven hours after water was allowed to flow back, Coffin's team could clearly see the first steelhead venturing into the new channel upstream from the old dam site. But there is another sign of success which Coffin is keen to reveal. **41** ____ The rounded stones on it range from the size of potatoes to loaves of bread, and make walking difficult. But Coffin is thrilled to see them because they are newly arrived, having just been washed in by the current.

The stones in the river provide nesting spots for the steelhead and a habitat for the insects that they eat. **42** ____ To illustrate this, he turns over a couple of rocks and points out six types of insect clinging to the underside, including caddisfly larvae and a stonefly. 'The year after the dam was removed, these wouldn't have been here,' he adds with satisfaction.

A The water there had become so shallow that it was possible for people to wade all the way across.

B 'People pay attention to the big fish,' Coffin says. 'Yes, they're an important part of the system, but they're not the only things.'

C One result of these projects has been an unanticipated research opportunity to study how to minimize the damage caused by releasing huge floods of water and decades of sediment.

D However, the reservoir lost its water and much of its mud, sand and gravel in three hours.

E Coffin leads me through patches of alder trees that were planted after the dam was removed, then crosses a rocky beach by the river.

F In the process of doing this, the workers rediscovered the river's original channel along the reservoir bottom.

G Built back in 1935, the structure provided power and irrigation for a nearby tree nursery that shut down in 1997.

Part 7

You are going to read an article in which four people talk about giving up successful careers to do something very different. For questions **43–52**, choose from the people (**A–D**). The people may be chosen more than once.

Mark your answers **on the separate answer sheet**.

Which person

is not always confident that they have done the right thing?	**43**	
is pleased to have proved doubters wrong?	**44**	
says they found success more easily in their first career than in their second?	**45**	
regrets not having changed careers sooner?	**46**	
refers to a time when they needed to gain confidence?	**47**	
mentions a sense of amazement when looking back at the past?	**48**	
admits that they changed career too suddenly?	**49**	
describes an urge to return to a childhood interest?	**50**	
says that skills developed in their first career proved useful?	**51**	
mentions feeling envious at one point?	**52**	

I gave up my career for something very different

A Mike Donne

I started doing magic tricks for family and friends when I was about seven, and by sixteen I was performing at big public events. I was also good academically, and studied law at university. Ten years after my degree, I was a busy lawyer with no time for magic, although I missed it. Then, out of the blue, a couple of old friends asked if I'd let them use some of my old material in a touring magic show they were setting up. I agreed but it bothered me that they were doing something I'd always loved, while I was in a job I had very little passion for. So, I joined them. I was very rusty initially, and I had to practise for several months before I felt able to perform in public, but I'm now one of the main acts. Funnily enough, it's been far tougher to make it as a magician than as a lawyer, but I've realised that this is what makes me feel alive.

B Kristina Mayer

I used to work for a bank and made enough from that to be in a position to buy my own apartment when I was 22. After a few years, however, dissatisfaction set in. I was just sitting at a computer, manipulating figures, and I longed to get out into the fresh air and move around. Then, one weekend, some friends talked me into going surfing with them. Surprisingly, it appealed to me so much that I ended up spending my days surfing and doing restaurant work in the evenings. I'm now taking part in competitions and I promote surf gear as a professional surfer. At times I can hardly afford to pay the rent, and I sometimes wonder whether leaving the bank was such a good idea, but then I remember I'm doing my favourite thing in the world.

C Carl Johnson

Five years ago I was an accountant, well-paid but feeling unfulfilled in my life. Then, my cousin asked if I'd help out at his burger restaurant one weekend when he was short of staff. I'd always liked burgers ever since I was small, but I was surprised at how much I enjoyed making them. Two weeks later I quit my job, hired a van and some equipment, and started selling burgers at street markets. It would've been better to have taken more time doing some proper background research, but what I knew about accounting came in handy, and my enthusiasm made up for my inexperience. I've now acquired a second van and taken on a couple of assistants, so the business is growing. It's incredible to think how much my life has changed.

D Agnes Porter

I was a very creative child, but I was taught that success lay in other directions. So I worked hard and ended up as human resources manager of an international company. It was well-paid but I dreamed of starting my own business. So during one holiday last year, I decided to experiment and made cakes for a couple of wedding receptions. They turned out to be very popular and, within a month, I'd resigned from my job and was making cakes full-time. Pushing myself hard to do well is in my nature, so I still work a lot, but I feel more in control of things now. People used to say that having my own business was an unrealistic dream, so demonstrating I could achieve it has been very satisfying. It's just a pity I didn't do it several years ago.

WRITING (1 hour 20 minutes)

Part 1

You **must** answer this question. Write your answer in **140–190** words in an appropriate style **on the separate answer sheet**.

---

1 In your English class you have been talking about advertising. Now, your English teacher has asked you to write an essay.

Write your essay using **all** the notes and giving reasons for your point of view.

'Advertising is a very good thing for society.' Do you agree?

Notes

Write about:

1. keeping people informed
2. encouraging competition between companies
3. .... (your own idea)

Part 2

Write an answer to **one** of the questions **2–4** in this part. Write your answer in **140–190** words in an appropriate style **on the separate answer sheet**. Put the question number in the box at the top of the answer sheet.

---

2 You see this notice in an English-language magazine:

> *Articles wanted*
>
> **Changes!**
>
> Some people love changes, others dislike them. What about you?
> Which changes in your life have had a big effect on you?
>
> The best articles will be printed next month.

Write your **article**.

3 This is an email you have received from your English-speaking friend, Marcus:

> **Subject: Learning English**
>
> Hi
> I'm researching the ways people learn English in different countries. Can you write and tell me about the most popular ways of learning English for people in your country?
> Write soon
> Marcus

Write your **email**.

4 You have seen this notice on a travel website:

> *Reviews wanted*
>
> **Guidebooks for tourists**
>
> We're looking for reviews of a good guidebook to your city or country.
>
> In your review you should include information about:
>
> - the contents of the book
> - what makes the book useful and interesting
> - why it's better than similar guidebooks.

Write your **review**.

LISTENING (approximately 40 minutes)

Part 1

You will hear people talking in eight different situations.

For questions **1–8**, choose the best answer (**A**, **B** or **C**).

---

1 You hear a young woman who is an apprentice cook talking about her apprenticeship.

How does she feel about it?

A grateful to be working in a four-star restaurant

B pleased that her teacher told her about the opportunity

C confident about fulfilling her ambitions

2 You hear two students talking about passing the time on bus journeys.

What technique for passing the time do they both sometimes use?

A listening to music

B observing the world outside

C concentrating on what's happening inside

3 You hear a cycle coach telling his group about the ride they are going to do.

What instruction does the coach give?

A Don't go too fast on the return route.

B Stick together on the main road.

C Don't take the first sign to the destination.

4 You hear part of an interview in which a writer talks about autobiographies.

What does the writer say about them?

A He prefers working on books about people he knows.

B He is unlikely to write one himself.

C He thinks the more popular ones are very boring.

5 You hear a journalist telling a colleague about her time at university.

How did she first get interested in journalism?

A by doing research online

B by accepting a chance request

C by reading a particularly interesting article

6 You hear a man and a woman talking about a new clothes shop they have visited.

What does the man say about having a member of staff to welcome customers?

A It seems like a worthwhile idea.

B Other people might appreciate it.

C Worse things happen in other shops.

7 You overhear a woman talking on the phone to a friend.

What is the woman talking about?

A an idea for a small short-term business

B the various career options open to her

C her role in a forthcoming expedition

8 You hear part of a broadcast on the radio.

What type of broadcast is it?

A a programme advertisement

B a wildlife documentary

C a news summary

Part 2

You will hear a woman called Paula Kanning, who works as a film advisor in local government, talking about her work. For questions **9–18**, complete the sentences with a word or short phrase.

Film Advisor

Paula's job title when she started working in the film department was **(9)** ....

Paula was first attracted to the job by the **(10)** .... on offer.

The most popular place for filmmakers in Paula's area is a **(11)** ....

Paula mentions a well-known advertisement for **(12)** .... that she proposed the site for.

Paula mentions that in her first year she sometimes needed to persuade **(13)** .... to agree to filming.

Paula is particularly proud of the **(14)** .... she built up during her first year in the department.

Paula's current job involves managing a project with the name **(15)** ....

Paula finds creating **(16)** .... for tourists the most difficult part of her current job.

Paula believes it is necessary to protect the **(17)** .... of local residents as well as their property.

Paula's department has recently set up what she calls a **(18)** .... scheme for students.

Part 3

You will hear five short extracts in which people talk about why they did not go to university directly after leaving school. For questions **19–23**, choose which of the reasons (**A–H**) each speaker gives. Use the letters only once. There are three extra letters which you do not need to use.

A a wish to see new places

B a misunderstanding about applying

C a desire to have a break from studying

D a wish to stay near to home

E a decision to prioritise family commitments

F a desire to start a career immediately

G a feeling of not being mature enough

H an inability to find a suitable course

Speaker 1		**19**
Speaker 2		**20**
Speaker 3		**21**
Speaker 4		**22**
Speaker 5		**23**

Part 4

You will hear a radio interview with a woman called Susan Fletcher, who works on a research station in Antarctica. For questions **24–30**, choose the best answer (**A**, **B** or **C**).

---

24 How does Susan feel before each trip to Antarctica?

A anxious because she'll miss people she cares about

B concerned about dealing with what lies ahead

C relieved to be leaving problems behind

25 Susan says that what's most stressful for her at the moment is

A not being able to predict everything you may need.

B not having enough time to prepare properly.

C not knowing exactly where she's going.

26 What does Susan admire about her colleagues?

A their scientific skills

B their lack of selfishness

C their success as researchers

27 Susan says the entertainment that's organised at the research station

A serves a useful purpose.

B allows people to show off their talents.

C disturbs people's regular schedules.

28 On the research station, Susan sometimes has difficulty

A getting enough time alone.

B eating the same food all the time.

C having a comfortable night's sleep.

29 What does Susan say she loves about her work?

A the chance to observe such fascinating wildlife

B being able to live so far from populated areas

C the fact that such a unique place is so familiar to her

30 Susan advises students hoping to work in Antarctica to

A make sure they have skills that are not purely academic.

B develop a high level of competence in their particular subject.

C think carefully about whether they're well-suited to the lifestyle.

SPEAKING (14 minutes)

You take the Speaking test with another candidate (possibly two candidates), referred to here as your partner. There are two examiners. One will speak to you and your partner and the other will be listening. Both examiners will award marks.

Part 1 (2 minutes)

The examiner asks you and your partner questions about yourselves. You may be asked about things like 'your home town', 'your interests', 'your career plans', etc.

Part 2 (a one-minute 'long turn' for each candidate, plus a 30-second response from the second candidate)

The examiner gives you two photographs and asks you to talk about them for one minute. The examiner then asks your partner a question about your photographs and your partner responds briefly.

Then the examiner gives your partner two different photographs. Your partner talks about these photographs for one minute. This time the examiner asks you a question about your partner's photographs and you respond briefly.

Part 3 (4 minutes)

The examiner asks you and your partner to talk together. They give you a task to look at so you can think about and discuss an idea, giving reasons for your opinion. For example, you may be asked to think about some changes in the world, or about spending free time with your family. After you have discussed the task for about two minutes with your partner, the examiner will ask you a follow-up question, which you should discuss for a further minute.

Part 4 (4 minutes)

The examiner asks some further questions, which leads to a more general discussion of what you have talked about in Part 3. You may comment on your partner's answers if you wish.

Test 4

READING AND USE OF ENGLISH (1 hour 15 minutes)

Part 1

For questions **1–8**, read the text below and decide which answer (**A**, **B**, **C** or **D**) best fits each gap. There is an example at the beginning (**0**).

Mark your answers **on the separate answer sheet**.

Example:

0 **A** points **B** marks **C** shows **D** finds

0	A	B	C	D
		(marked)		

An ancient cave interests scientists

At the base of a hill in South Africa, a cluster of huge stones **(0)** .... the entrance to one of humanity's oldest known dwelling places. In fact, humans have **(1)** .... Wonderwerk Cave for 2 million years – most recently in the early 1900s, when a farming family **(2)** .... it their home. Wonderwerk holds another distinction as well: the cave contains the earliest **(3)** .... evidence that our ancient ancestors were using fire for cooking.

Like many archaeological finds, this one was accidental. Researchers were trying to **(4)** .... the age of primitive stone tools that had been unearthed in the cave. In the process, they **(5)** .... across the ashes of a campfire containing what turned **(6)** .... to be remains of food from a million years ago. That was 200,000 years older than any **(7)** .... discovered remnants of human-controlled fire. At Wonderwerk, the researchers are digging ever deeper, analysing soil up to 1.8 million years old, **(8)** .... evidence of even older fires.

1	**A**	occupied	**B**	stayed	**C**	settled	**D**	remained
2	**A**	built	**B**	found	**C**	used	**D**	made
3	**A**	heavy	**B**	fixed	**C**	solid	**D**	dense
4	**A**	conclude	**B**	detect	**C**	notice	**D**	determine
5	**A**	came	**B**	looked	**C**	went	**D**	fell
6	**A**	out	**B**	in	**C**	off	**D**	back
7	**A**	last	**B**	previously	**C**	once	**D**	formerly
8	**A**	enquiring	**B**	looking	**C**	seeking	**D**	chasing

Part 2

For questions **9–16**, read the text below and think of the word which best fits each gap. Use only one word in each gap. There is an example at the beginning (**0**).

Write your answers **IN CAPITAL LETTERS on the separate answer sheet**.

Example: | 0 | | O | F |

The joys of horse riding

For me, riding a horse is a delightful combination **(0)** .... adventure, excitement and relaxation. You can proceed at a slow, peaceful trot **(9)** .... choose to go at full speed, **(10)** .... you prefer that. **(11)** .... I love most about being on a horse is that you get a different view of the world, seeing things you would not normally see, totally surrounded by nature. Each ride has **(12)** .... own appeal. I especially cherish cold, crisp days in winter when the ground sparkles with snow. Even riding in the rain has a certain appeal – splashing through puddles and galloping home quickly so **(13)** .... to escape the next downpour. **(14)** .... paths you ride along may be familiar, you can never quite predict the surprises beyond the next corner. Riding alone can be fabulous, but going out on horses with a friend is best of **(15)** .... Even the horses seem to enjoy the company of each **(16)** ....

Part 3

For questions **17–24**, read the text below. Use the word given in capitals at the end of some of the lines to form a word that fits in the gap **in the same line**. There is an example at the beginning **(0)**.

Write your answers **IN CAPITAL LETTERS on the separate answer sheet.**

Example: | **0** | D | E | V | E | L | O | P | M | E | N | T |

Henry Ford

One of the most important contributions of the American	
businessman, Henry Ford to the **(0)** .... of the automobile was	**DEVELOP**
as inventor of the moving assembly line in 1913. Before this,	
teams of factory workers would all work together to construct	
a complete car. With an assembly line, each **(17)** .... in	**EMPLOY**
Ford's factory had a specific **(18)** .... for only one job when	**RESPONSIBLE**
putting together the car. This **(19)** .... of labour resulted in	**DIVIDE**
(20) .... cost savings and meant that the total time taken in	**SIGNIFY**
producing the cars was shortened quite **(21)** .... With the addition	**CONSIDER**
of an **(22)** .... system for moving the cars as they were being	**INNOVATE**
assembled, Ford's factory turned out a finished car every 93 minutes.	
Even then, cars were too **(23)** .... for most people. Therefore, Ford	**COST**
raised the minimum wage for his factory workers which led to general	
wage increases across America. In this way, cars became **(24)**	**AFFORD**
for more people and therefore relatively inexpensive compared to	
previous times.	

Part 4

For questions **25–30**, complete the second sentence so that it has a similar meaning to the first sentence, using the word given. **Do not change the word given**. You must use between **two** and **five** words, including the word given. Here is an example (**0**).

Example:

0 A very friendly taxi driver drove us into town.

DRIVEN

We .... a very friendly taxi driver.

The gap can be filled by the words 'were driven into town by', so you write:

Example:

0	*WERE DRIVEN INTO TOWN BY*

Write **only** the missing words **IN CAPITAL LETTERS on the separate answer sheet**.

---

25 Thick fog prevented the plane from landing.

UNABLE

The plane .... of the thick fog.

26 Mr Brown was just about to leave home when he remembered he hadn't bought a ticket.

POINT

Mr Brown was .... home when he remembered he hadn't bought a ticket.

27 I first visited Rome ten years ago.

SINCE

It has .... first visit to Rome.

28 Helen didn't tell me anything about the interview she had yesterday.

WORD

Helen .... to me about the interview she had yesterday.

29 Membership of the club is open to anyone over eighteen.

AGE

Anyone who is more than eighteen .. .. a member of the club.

30 Carole is hardly ever late for work.

ALMOST

Carole is .... time for work.

Part 5

You are going to read an article by Cal Flynn, who went to the Arctic Circle to work for a company that runs husky sled trips. For questions **31–36**, choose the answer (**A**, **B**, **C** or **D**) which you think fits best according to the text.

Mark your answers **on the separate answer sheet**.

Working with huskies

Just over a year ago, I left my job to work with huskies in the Arctic Circle in the far north of Finland. At 26, I was restless. I was dreaming of Arctic landscapes, cold and bleak expanses, perhaps in reaction to the noise and crowded living of London. So I found a small company run by Anna McCormack, and her husband, Pasi Ikonen, deep in Finnish Lapland. They agreed to take me on as a husky dog handler for a busy winter season. From December to February, there is plenty of business taking tourists out on sled rides pulled by huskies across the ice and snow (for anything from an hour to a five-day stretch). They started with six dogs, which rapidly expanded to more than 100.

Recently, they took over a second property – the 'wilderness farm', which they wrote was a picturesque but basic outpost with untrustworthy electrics and no running water. I could join the team for three months, they told me, if I knew what I was letting myself in for. 'The hours are long, the conditions tough and the work very physical.' I started packing straight away.

November 6, London

On my flight out I look out of the window. It is said that spring marches north at a rate of about 26 km per day, a tidal wave of opening flowers and leaves. I think what I am seeing, however, is the opposite movement, with winter marching south, and the rivers freezing over.

November 7, Helsinki and Hetta

We drive north by bus through endless dark forest – thin conifers, weighed down by snow – stopping occasionally to let reindeer lumber out of the way. I arrive at the farm after dark, and am barely through the door when I'm handed a pair of boots and turned out into the cold. 'Do you want to be thrown in at the deep end?' Anna asks. It's a rhetorical question.

I follow the sound of barking, which grows to a wall of noise by the time I reach the dogsheds. Three figures are running back and forth up the lines of huskies, pulling them out and harnessing them to sleds. The dogs are almost hysterical with excitement, straining against the ropes in their desperation to be off. I can barely hear to introduce myself, but the others are too harried to stop and talk much anyway. I hover on the sidelines and rub the forehead of one of the quieter dogs. Someone gestures at me impatiently – 'Get in!' – and I almost fall into the nearest sled. A command rings out, and with a jerk we are off into the dark, with only a head torch for light.

November 15, Hetta

It does not take long to be initiated into the ranks of the husky guides. 'Are you useful?' Anna asks. I'm stumped. I don't know. Am I? Further questioning reveals that no, I am not: I have never driven a snowmobile, haven't done woodwork since school and have never chopped anything with an axe. 'You do have a driving licence?' someone asks finally. I nod, relieved.

The basics of dog-sledding can be picked up very quickly: lean into the corners, put both feet on the brake to stop, and, whatever happens, don't let go of the handlebar. But everything else seems to be very complicated. Simple tasks such as feeding and watering the dogs become very difficult in sub-zero conditions. A bowl of water will freeze solid while you watch, so we must make a 'soup' of meat in hot water for the dogs. By the end of my first week my head is going round and round after so many instructions and my muscles ache from dragging heavy sleds – and from being dragged around myself by overenthusiastic huskies. But I am triumphant. 'I can chop with an axe, hammer a nail, and use a circular saw,' I email friends excitedly. 'In the snow.'

31 What were Cal's feelings when leaving London?

A convinced she needed to be somewhere more relaxing
B happy to further her knowledge of the tourism industry
C looking forward to helping Anna and Pasi build their business
D longing for a contrast to her current lifestyle

32 What was Cal's reaction to the description of the farm?

A put off by its remoteness
B enthusiastic about taking on its challenges
C hopeful of extending her stay
D attracted to the idea of being part of a group

33 Cal uses the phrase 'thrown in at the deep end' in line 41 to indicate that she was

A pushed into thick layers of snow.
B expected to swim in deep icy water.
C given something demanding to do initially.
D asked to do more work than others.

34 What does 'harried' mean in line 51?

A pressured
B exhausted
C silenced
D irritated

35 What impression is given of life with the husky guides?

A There is a welcoming atmosphere.
B There is an unnecessary level of aggression.
C People focus on getting the job done.
D People are expected to wait around without complaining.

36 How does Cal describe her situation after a week?

A She finds certain tasks easier than she'd been told they would be.
B She is resentful of the curiosity shown by others about her character.
C She feels confused by all the things she has been told to do.
D She is dissatisfied with her achievements.

Part 6

You are going to read an article about a charitable project that feeds a million school children. Six sentences have been removed from the article. Choose from the sentences **A–G** the one which fits each gap (**37–42**). There is one extra sentence which you do not need to use.

Mark your answers **on the separate answer sheet.**

The man who organised meals for children all over the world from his garden shed

In a remote Scottish valley stands a small iron shed that is affecting the lives of a million children thousands of kilometres away. The shed was the birthplace in 2002 of a tiny charity called Mary's Meals, run by a man called Magnus MacFarlane-Barrow. Magnus now employs fifty people in the Scottish city of Glasgow, but continues to work from the shed himself.

Magnus used to work for a large humanitarian organisation, and this job took him all over the world. During one trip in 2002, he was being shown round a school by a local teacher, when he asked a young boy of 14 what his dreams were. The boy said, 'to have enough food to eat and to go to school.' **37** He would provide dinner for them each day they were at school.

As he researched it over a lengthy period, Magnus found that many children around the world were going to school without having had any breakfast, 'and they weren't getting anything at school – so it would be evening before they got fed,' Magnus says. **38**

At the last count, Mary's Meals was working in 1,300 schools in 12 countries across four continents, providing school meals to 996,926 children each day. 'You find that when school dinners are provided, enrolment increases by around 18% – in some instances it's a lot more and the school roll has doubled in a matter of weeks,' says Magnus. **39** 'And attendance rates go up too, because in many schools children are enrolled but don't attend school very often, and that changes once they know they will be fed. And academic performance also improves a lot – because now not only are children coming in to school, they are also not hungry in lessons.'

The successes are all the more remarkable given the fact that it costs relatively little to feed a child for a whole school year. While Mary's Meals has grown dramatically, it has a modest income in comparison with other charities. **40** The school feeding programmes are run by local communities. Mary's Meals works to establish links with local farmers and community leaders such as teachers. These people organise a small army of volunteers, most of them mothers, who cook and serve the meals. Mary's Meals provides the kitchen, with all the cooking equipment. It also pays for the locally sourced food and gives training.

In 2012 one young supporter of Mary's Meals, nine year-old Martha Payne, catapulted the charity to new heights of fame when she started a fundraising blog about her own unhealthy school dinners in Scotland and was briefly banned from doing so by her local council. **41** The decision was soon reversed after protests on the internet.

Magnus's main focus, however, remains more global. **42** There are, he says, an enormous number of children across the world who are not in school because of hunger and poverty. 'In many ways, I feel we are just beginning.'

A This was an idea of brilliant simplicity, but proved complex to put into practice.

B The sums involved are still enough to have a significant impact, though.

C He felt that was an intolerable situation and knew that changing it would make a big difference.

D The incident attracted a lot of attention, which Magnus admits was not unwelcome.

E Magnus realised there and then that there was one relatively simple intervention that could transform life for children all over the developing world.

F He is delighted with the way things have gone so far, but says there's a great deal that remains to be done.

G 'In the short term that can be problematic, but in the long term it's fantastic,' he adds.

Part 7

You are going to read a magazine article about being a journalist. For questions **43–52**, choose from the sections (**A–D**). The sections may be chosen more than once.

Mark your answers **on the separate answer sheet**.

In which section does the writer mention

having to rely on others when researching a story?	**43**	
how inspiration for articles can come from listening to people's conversations?	**44**	
some views on the state of the profession?	**45**	
the need to have realistic expectations?	**46**	
the pressure of having to meet deadlines?	**47**	
the importance of analysing what makes a good article?	**48**	
getting a sense of satisfaction from the responses of readers?	**49**	
the advantages of establishing positive relationships with other journalists?	**50**	
variety being a benefit of working as a journalist?	**51**	
the degree of preparation involved in producing different articles?	**52**	

So you want to become a journalist?

Susannah Butter tells us what being a journalist is really like.

A

A journalist's life can be hectic. The morning is usually the busiest part of the day because the newspaper I work on has to be ready for printing by noon. I work on the features pages – that is, on longer articles, often about interesting people's lives, which requires a lot of thought and organisation. With some of our articles we can take time to think, do proper research and write them in advance. Whereas others are more urgent, timely pieces with a quick turnaround. I'm sometimes asked to write a story that's needed for the next day. It can be scary knowing you have to find lots of information, write around 1,000 words and get ideas for pictures in just a few hours. I like digging up stuff that hasn't been reported and then presenting it in a way that readers will understand and value. It's great when you see people reading and enjoying a piece you've written. At all times, you need to think about how a story can be sold – for example, what accompanying picture and headline will draw people in.

B

Writing an article can involve having to find people's addresses and knocking on doors to ask them questions. My job allows me to meet and talk to a huge range of interesting people, and it changes all the time. In just one week, I might be working on an interview with a singer, a piece about coffee shops and an investigation into an unsolved crime. I think I'd get bored working on one thing all the time! My least favourite thing is probably chasing people for answers – this can involve a long chain of people that eventually leads you to the one person you want to write about. You have to be patient and persistent, politely reminding people what you want and when. You have to know just how far you can push them.

C

Pursuing a career in journalism was a natural choice for me because I'd always read newspapers and been quite nosy about other people's lives. At university, I did a bit of student journalism, editing the arts pages of a student newspaper and doing some writing. In my final year, I went to a careers talk about journalism. After I graduated, I emailed the journalist I'd met at the talk and asked her for work experience. I got it and really enjoyed it. People kept telling me that print journalism was dead, that there's no money in it in the age of the internet. But I figured that I'd give it a go anyway. I decided to take it seriously and get as qualified as I could. I've never regretted it.

D

For those considering a career in journalism, I would recommend reading as much as you can and keeping your eyes and ears open in everyday situations, which is great for getting ideas for stories. You also need to think about articles which work well and why, and remember this when you sit down to write your own. Being a good writer is an advantage, but in my experience journalism is as much about having new ideas and getting things done (preferably quickly!). But don't assume you will be writing front-page stories, or even having your name on any articles at first. Initially, it's about getting to know the people and the system. If they like you, they're more likely to give you an interesting task, listen to your ideas or give you advice.

WRITING (1 hour 20 minutes)

Part 1

You **must** answer this question. Write your answer in **140–190** words in an appropriate style **on the separate answer sheet**.

---

1 In your English class you have been talking about long-lasting products. Now, your English teacher has asked you to write an essay.

Write your essay using **all** the notes and giving reasons for your point of view.

Is it a good or bad thing to have products that last a long time?

Notes

Write about:

1. changing technology
2. fashion
3. .... (your own idea)

Part 2

Write an answer to **one** of the questions **2–4** in this part. Write your answer in **140–190** words in an appropriate style **on the separate answer sheet**. Put the question number in the box at the top of the answer sheet.

---

2 In your English class you have been discussing the leisure activities, for example sports and clubs, available at your college. Your English teacher has now asked you to write a report.

In your report, you should:

- describe the current leisure facilities and activities in your college
- explain what improvements you would like to see
- say why these improvements would be popular with students.

Write your **report**.

3 You have seen this notice in an English online magazine:

> *Reviews wanted*
>
> **Interesting Exhibitions**
>
> Have you been to an interesting exhibition recently? It could have been about art, photography, science or another subject. Write us a review:
>
> - describing the exhibition
> - explaining why you found it interesting
> - saying which people you would recommend it to.
>
> The best reviews will appear on the website.

Write your **review**.

4 You see this advertisement in a travel magazine:

> **Wanted: Walking guides**
>
> We are looking for people to take tourist groups walking in your area. You should:
>
> - have a broad knowledge of the countryside in your area
> - have experience of walking 15+ kms a day
> - be a good communicator in English.
>
> To apply, write to the project organiser, Ms Sally Morley, explaining why you are suitable for the job.

Write your **letter of application**

LISTENING (approximately 40 minutes)

Part 1

You will hear people talking in eight different situations.

For questions **1–8**, choose the best answer (**A**, **B** or **C**).

---

1 You hear a man talking about an ancient object he found in the ground.

The man took the object to a museum because

A he thought it might be valuable.

B he decided to record his find.

C he wanted to know what it was.

2 You hear two friends talking about advertising.

What does the woman say about advertisements?

A They are merely a form of entertainment.

B They make people buy things they don't need.

C They give people misleading information about new products.

3 You hear an actor talking about her career.

What does she say about how she became an actor?

A She had a chance meeting with someone.

B She was successful at drama school.

C She asked her friend to help her.

4 You hear a tour guide telling a group of tourists about a view.

Which feature does the guide think will be most familiar to them?

A the park

B the river

C the wood

5 You hear a man talking to a friend about a presentation he has just given.

How does he feel now?

A relieved that the audience was small

B confident that he spoke clearly

C surprised that so many people asked questions

6 You hear two students talking about a careers talk they have just heard at college.

What do they disagree about?

A how useful the information was

B how entertaining the speaker was

C how well the audience behaved

7 You hear an author of children's books talking about her work.

What point is she making?

A She wants her books to be educational.

B Her books are about her real-life experiences.

C Friendship is the main focus of her stories.

8 You hear a man and a woman talking about older people learning languages.

What does the man say about them?

A They don't take advantage of technology.

B They have more time to study.

C They use better learning techniques.

Part 2

You will hear a student called Andy Richards talking about his recent trip to the tea growing region of Assam in Northern India. For questions **9–18**, complete the sentences with a word or short phrase.

Visit to a tea plantation

As part of his **(9)** .... course at university, Andy went to India to gather information for a project.

Andy compares the tea plant's growing conditions to a **(10)** ....

Andy's group were invited to the **(11)** .... for the tea tasting session.

Andy was surprised that, as well as the leaves, the tea pickers also picked the **(12)** .... of the plants.

On the elephant ride, Andy was able to see the **(13)** .... in the distance.

At the tea party, the **(14)** .... particularly impressed Andy.

When going over a **(15)** .... , Andy nearly fell off his motorbike.

In the market, Andy was very surprised to see the **(16)** .... on sale.

Andy was pleased with the price he paid for the **(17)** .... for his sister.

The **(18)** .... were Andy's favourite vegetables out of all those on display at the market.

Part 3

You will hear five short extracts in which people are talking about work they did in shops. For questions **19–23**, choose from the options (**A–H**) what each person says about their experience. Use the letters only once. There are three extra letters which you do not need to use.

A My confidence was sometimes affected by customers' attitudes.

B I was pleased to discover that I had a good way with customers.

C It made me appreciate the people I worked with.

D The training I received didn't equip me to do my job well.

E Customers were satisfied when they got a bargain.

F I wasn't happy with some of the products in the shop.

G It was motivating to sell more than the other assistants.

H It exhausted me both physically and mentally.

Speaker 1		**19**
Speaker 2		**20**
Speaker 3		**21**
Speaker 4		**22**
Speaker 5		**23**

Part 4

You will hear an interview with Marvin Benby, a beekeeper who keeps his bees in hives on a city rooftop. For questions **24–30**, choose the best answer (**A**, **B** or **C**).

---

24 What made Marvin get into beekeeping?

A He was persuaded to try it by a friend.

B A friend offered to teach him about it.

C He wanted to prove a friend wrong.

25 Marvin thinks the best part about keeping bees is

A helping to increase the bee population.

B the excitement of checking his beehives.

C having access to so much honey.

26 One of the difficulties for Marvin of city beekeeping is

A taking it personally when things go wrong.

B ensuring the bees get to a variety of flowers.

C getting hold of the most suitable equipment.

27 Marvin says that one of his neighbours

A complained about being stung by a bee.

B insisted that Marvin moved his beehives.

C had concerns due to an allergy to bees.

28 When Marvin set up his first beehive

A he became confused about what to do.

B he made some potentially dangerous mistakes.

C his bees became nervous and stressed.

29 What does Marvin say about selling bee-related products?

A He has started to make a profit.

B Local people are starting to buy them.

C It cost him a lot to get started.

30 How does Marvin feel about the next few months?

A He has a mixture of contrasting feelings.

B He hopes to enjoy a more relaxed period.

C He is confident that he can manage.

SPEAKING (14 minutes)

You take the Speaking test with another candidate (possibly two candidates), referred to here as your partner. There are two examiners. One will speak to you and your partner and the other will be listening. Both examiners will award marks.

Part 1 (2 minutes)

The examiner asks you and your partner questions about yourselves. You may be asked about things like 'your home town', 'your interests', 'your career plans', etc.

Part 2 (a one-minute 'long turn' for each candidate, plus a 30-second response from the second candidate)

The examiner gives you two photographs and asks you to talk about them for one minute. The examiner then asks your partner a question about your photographs and your partner responds briefly.

Then the examiner gives your partner two different photographs. Your partner talks about these photographs for one minute. This time the examiner asks you a question about your partner's photographs and you respond briefly.

Part 3 (4 minutes)

The examiner asks you and your partner to talk together. They give you a task to look at so you can think about and discuss an idea, giving reasons for your opinion. For example, you may be asked to think about some changes in the world, or about spending free time with your family. After you have discussed the task for about two minutes with your partner, the examiner will ask you a follow-up question, which you should discuss for a further minute.

Part 4 (4 minutes)

The examiner asks some further questions, which leads to a more general discussion of what you have talked about in Part 3. You may comment on your partner's answers if you wish.

CAMBRIDGE ENGLISH
Language Assessment
Part of the University of Cambridge

Do not write in this box

SAMPLE

Candidate Name
If not already printed, write name in CAPITALS and complete the Candidate No. grid (in pencil).

Candidate Signature

Examination Title

Centre

Supervisor:
If the candidate is ABSENT or has WITHDRAWN shade here

Centre No.

Candidate No.

Examination Details

0	0	0	0
1	1	1	1
2	2	2	2
3	3	3	3
4	4	4	4
5	5	5	5
6	6	6	6
7	7	7	7
8	8	8	8
9	9	9	9

Candidate Answer Sheet

Instructions

Use a PENCIL (B or HB).

Rub out any answer you wish to change using an eraser.

Parts 1, 5, 6 and 7:
Mark ONE letter for each question.

For example, if you think **B** is the right answer to the question, mark your answer sheet like this:

0	A	B	C	D

Parts 2, 3 and 4:
Write your answer clearly in CAPITAL LETTERS.

For Parts 2 and 3 write one letter in each box. For example:

0	E	X	A	M	P	L	E

Part 1

1	A	B	C	D
2	A	B	C	D
3	A	B	C	D
4	A	B	C	D
5	A	B	C	D
6	A	B	C	D
7	A	B	C	D
8	A	B	C	D

Part 2

Do not write below here

																	Do not write below here
9																	9 1 0 u
10																	10 1 0 u
11																	11 1 0 u
12																	12 1 0 u
13																	13 1 0 u
14																	14 1 0 u
15																	15 1 0 u
16																	16 1 0 u

Continues over →

FCE R DP802

Part 3

		Do not write below here
17		17 1 0 u
18		18 1 0 u
19		19 1 0 u
20		20 1 0 u
21		21 1 0 u
22		22 1 0 u
23		23 1 0 u
24		24 1 0 u

Part 4

		Do not write below here
25		25 2 1 0 u
26		26 2 1 0 u
27		27 2 1 0 u
28		28 2 1 0 u
29		29 2 1 0 u
30		30 2 1 0 u

Part 5

31	A	B	C	D
32	A	B	C	D
33	A	B	C	D
34	A	B	C	D
35	A	B	C	D
36	A	B	C	D

Part 6

37	A	B	C	D	E	F	G
38	A	B	C	D	E	F	G
39	A	B	C	D	E	F	G
40	A	B	C	D	E	F	G
41	A	B	C	D	E	F	G
42	A	B	C	D	E	F	G

Part 7

43	A	B	C	D	E	F
44	A	B	C	D	E	F
45	A	B	C	D	E	F
46	A	B	C	D	E	F
47	A	B	C	D	E	F
48	A	B	C	D	E	F
49	A	B	C	D	E	F
50	A	B	C	D	E	F
51	A	B	C	D	E	F
52	A	B	C	D	E	F

CAMBRIDGE ENGLISH
Language Assessment
Part of the University of Cambridge

Do not write in this box

SAMPLE

Candidate Name
If not already printed, write name in CAPITALS and complete the Candidate No. grid (in pencil).

Candidate Signature

Examination Title

Centre

Supervisor:
If the candidate is ABSENT or has WITHDRAWN shade here

Centre No.

Candidate No.

Examination Details

0	0	0	0
1	1	1	1
2	2	2	2
3	3	3	3
4	4	4	4
5	5	5	5
6	6	6	6
7	7	7	7
8	8	8	8
9	9	9	9

Candidate Answer Sheet

Instructions

Use a PENCIL (B or HB).
Rub out any answer you wish to change using an eraser.

Parts 1, 3 and 4:
Mark ONE letter for each question.

For example, if you think **B** is the right answer to the question, mark your answer sheet like this:

0 A B C

Part 2:
Write your answer clearly in CAPITAL LETTERS.

Write one letter or number in each box.
If the answer has more than one word, leave one box empty between words.

For example:

0 AN EXAMPLE

Turn this sheet over to start.

Part 1

1	A	B	C
2	A	B	C
3	A	B	C
4	A	B	C
5	A	B	C
6	A	B	C
7	A	B	C
8	A	B	C

Part 2 (Remember to write in CAPITAL LETTERS or numbers)

		Do not write below here
9		9 1 0 u
10		10 1 0 u
11		11 1 0 u
12		12 1 0 u
13		13 1 0 u
14		14 1 0 u
15		15 1 0 u
16		16 1 0 u
17		17 1 0 u
18		18 1 0 u

Part 3

19	A	B	C	D	E	F	G	H
20	A	B	C	D	E	F	G	H
21	A	B	C	D	E	F	G	H
22	A	B	C	D	E	F	G	H
23	A	B	C	D	E	F	G	H

Part 4

24	A	B	C
25	A	B	C
26	A	B	C
27	A	B	C
28	A	B	C
29	A	B	C
30	A	B	C

Acknowledgements

The authors and publishers acknowledge the following sources of copyright material and are grateful for the permissions granted. While every effort has been made, it has not always been possible to identify the sources of all the material used, or to trace all copyright holders. If any omissions are brought to our notice, we will be happy to include the appropriate acknowledgements on reprinting and in the next update to the digital edition, as applicable.

Key: T = Top; B = Below.

Text

Heston Blumenthal for the text on p. 14 adapted from In Search of Total Perfection by Heston Blumenthal. Published by Bloomsbury. Copyright © 2009 Henston Blumenthal. Reproduced by permission of the author c/o Rogers, Colerdige & White Ltd. 20 Powis Mews, London W11 1JN; Travel Mamas for the text on p. 16 adapted from 'Swimming with Manatees, Florida's Gentle Giants' by Bel Kembach, 25.04.2017. Copyright © 2017 Travel Mamas. Reproduced with kind permission; Guardian News & Media Limited for the text on p. 19 adapted from 'Madagascar's fishing villagers learn to survive by managing their stocks' by Kit Buchan, The Guardian, 05.05.2015. Copyright © Guardian News and Media Limited 2015. Reproduced with permission; Guardian News & Media Limited for the text on p. 19 adapted from 'Cheap solar lamps help villagers keep their health, and cut emissions' by Katie Forster, The Guardian, 05.05.2015. Copyright © Guardian News and Media Limited 2015. Reproduced with permission; Guardian News & Media Limited for the text on p. 19 adapted from 'Vietnam cities told that driving down pollution is a matter of ride-sharing' by Kit Buchan, The Guardian, 05.05.2015. Copyright © Guardian News and Media Limited 2015. Reproduced with permission; Guardian News & Media Limited for the text on p. 19 adapted from 'Ghanas's bicycle which is creating jobs while it saves the soil' by Corinne Jones, The Guardian, 05.05.2015. Copyright © Guardian News and Media Limited 2015. Reproduced with permission; Guardian News & Media Limited for the text on p. 36 adapted from 'How do I become…a guitar maker?' by Sandra Haurant, The Guardian, 18.11.2015. Copyright © Guardian News and Media Limited 2015. Reproduced with permission; Guardian News & Media Limited for the text on p. 38 adapted from 'The BBC's Operation Iceberg captures a brief moment frozen in time' by Helen Czerski, The Guardian, 29.10.2012. Copyright © Guardian News and Media Limited 2012. Reproduced with permission; Telegraph Media Group Limited for the text on p. 41 adapted from 'Follow your animal instincts to keep fit' by Annabel Vennin, The Telegraph, 29.11.2014. Copyright © 2014 Telegraph Media Group Limited. Reproduced with permission; Telegraph Media Group Limited for the text on p. 58 adapted from 'Brother of all challenges for Alistair Brownlee' by Dominic Utton, The Telegraph, 13.02.2015. Copyright © 2015 Telegraph Media Group Limited. Reproduced with permission; Macmillan Publishers Limited for the text on p. 60 adapted from 'Dam removals: Rivers on the run' by Richard A. Lovett, Nature Vol. 511 Issue 7511, 30.07.2014. Copyright © 2014 Macmillan Publishers Limited. Reproduced with permission via the Copyright Clearance Center; Guardian News & Media Limited for the text on p. 63 adapted from 'What is it like to quit your life and start again?' by Becky Barnicoat and Chris Broughton, The Guardian, 12.06.2015. Copyright © Guardian News and Media Limited 2015. Reproduced with permission; Kalmbach Publishing Co. for the text on p. 74 from 'Archaeologists Find Earliest Evidence of Humans Cooking With Fire' by Kenneth Miller, 17.12.2013. Copyright © 2013 Kalmbach Publishing Co. Reproduced with kind permission; Telegraph Media Group Limited for the text on p. 80 adapted from 'My winter on a husky farm in the Arctic Circle' by Cal Flyn, The Telegraph, 20.12.2013. Copyright © Telegraph Media Group Limited. Reproduced with permission; Guardian News & Media Limited for the text on p. 82 from 'The man who feeds the developing world's children from a garden shed' by Joanna Moorhead, 17.05.2015. Copyright © Guardian News & Media Limited 2015. Reproduced with permission; Susannah Butter for the text on p. 85 from 'A day in the life of … An Evening Standard journalist' by Susannah Butter, The Reading Agency website. Copyright © 2013 Susannah Butter. Reproduced with kind permission.

Photos

All the photographs are sourced from Getty Images.

p. C1 (T): Witold Skrypczak/Witold Skrypczak; p. C1 (B): Daniel Allan/Daniel Allan; p. C2 (T): FRED TANNEAU/AFP; p. C2 (B): Ascent/PKS Media Inc./The Image Bank; p. C4 (T): Richard Baker/In Pictures p. C4 (B): Maskot; p. C5 (T): Katrina Wittkamp/DigitalVision; p. C5 (B), p. C8 (B): Hero Images; p. C7 (T): Monty Rakusen/Cultura; p. C7 (B): PeopleImages/DigitalVision; p. C8 (T): Chris Cross/Caiaimage; p. C10 (T): Jordan Siemens/DigitalVision; p. C10 (B): Image Source; p. C11 (T): franckreporter/E+; p. C11 (B): Glowimages.

Visual materials for the Speaking test

Why are the people getting information about these things?

1A

1B

Why are the people walking in these places?

1C

1D

1E

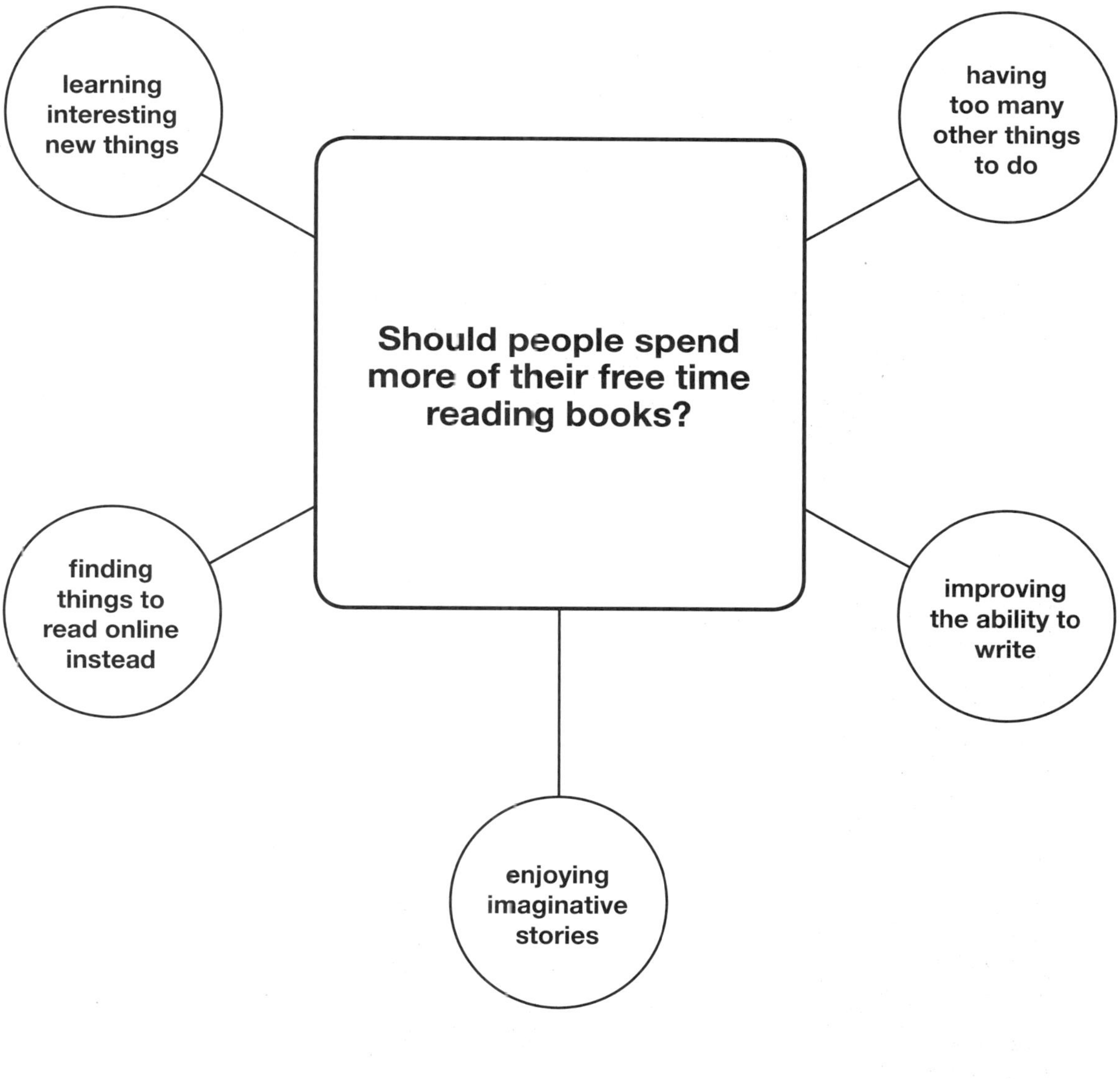
Should people spend more of their free time reading books?
learning interesting new things
having too many other things to do
finding things to read online instead
improving the ability to write
enjoying imaginative stories

What are the people enjoying about spending their holidays in these ways?

2A

2B

What might the people find difficult about choosing things in these situations?

2C

2D

2E

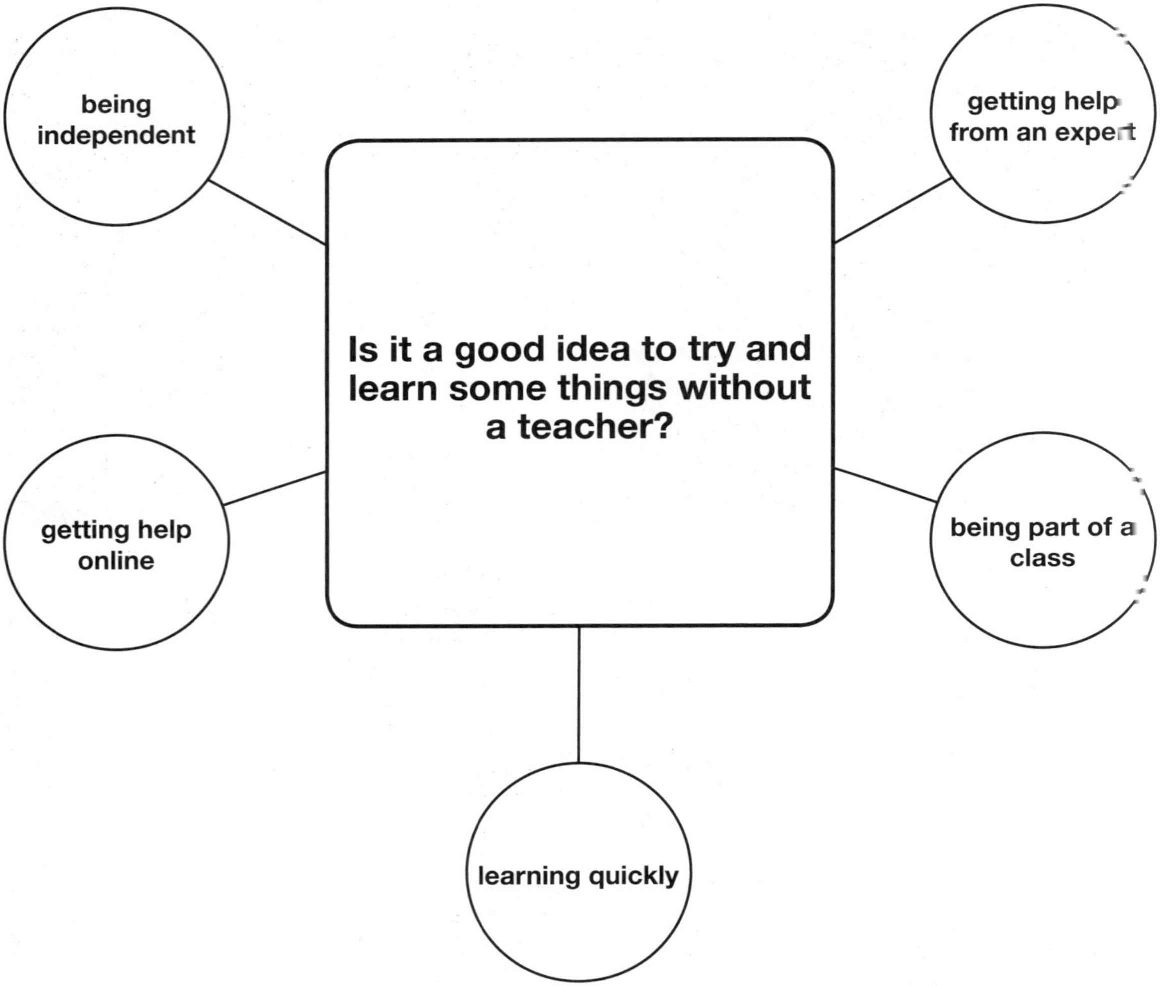
being independent
getting help from an expert
Is it a good idea to try and learn some things without a teacher?
getting help online
being part of a class
learning quickly

Why have the people decided to use their phores in these situations?

3A

3B

What are the people enjoying about doing these winter activities?

3C

3D

3E

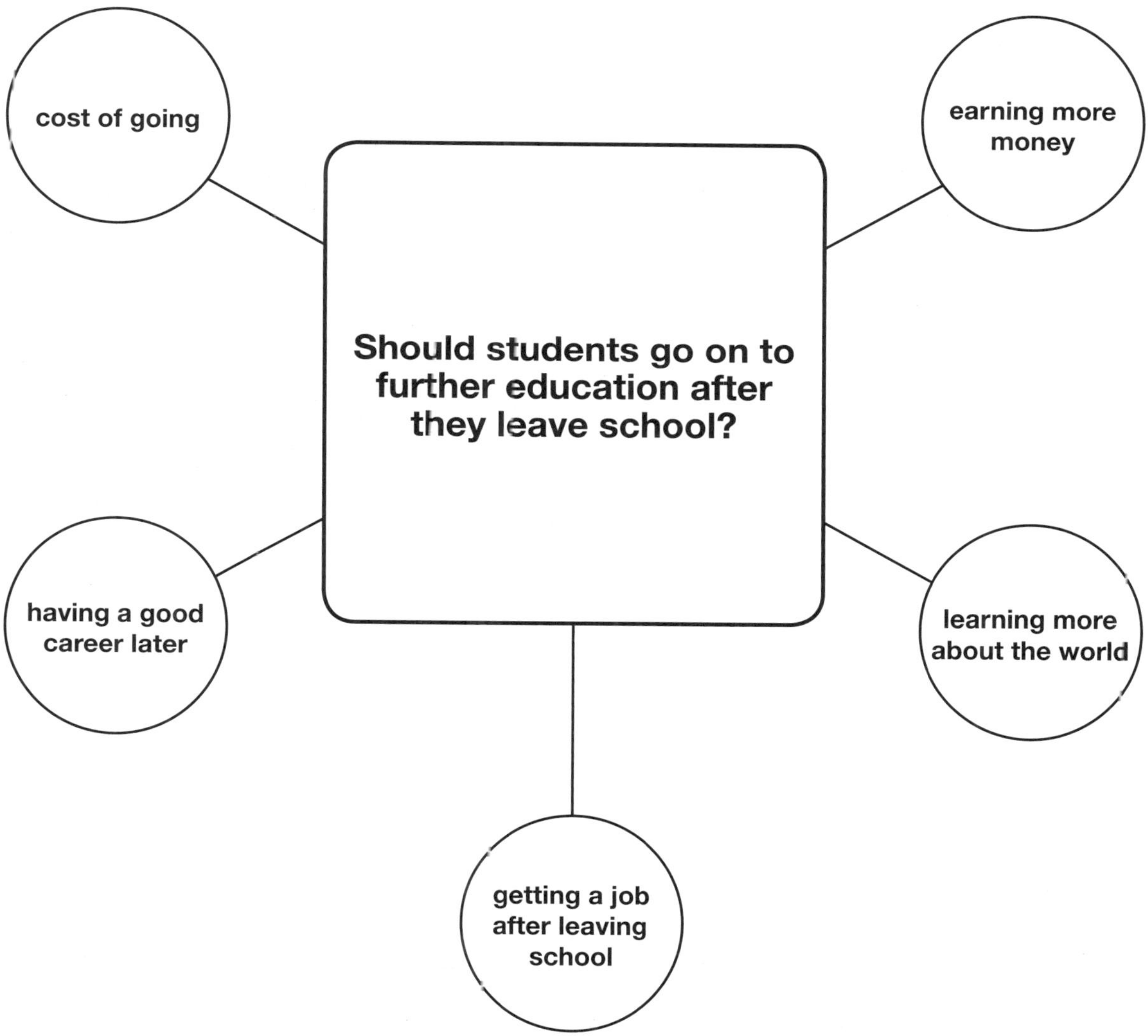
Should students go on to further education after they leave school?
cost of going
earning more money
having a good career later
learning more about the world
getting a job after leaving school

What are the people enjoying about spending time in these beautiful places?

4A

4B

Why are the people listening to music in these situations?

4C

4D

4E

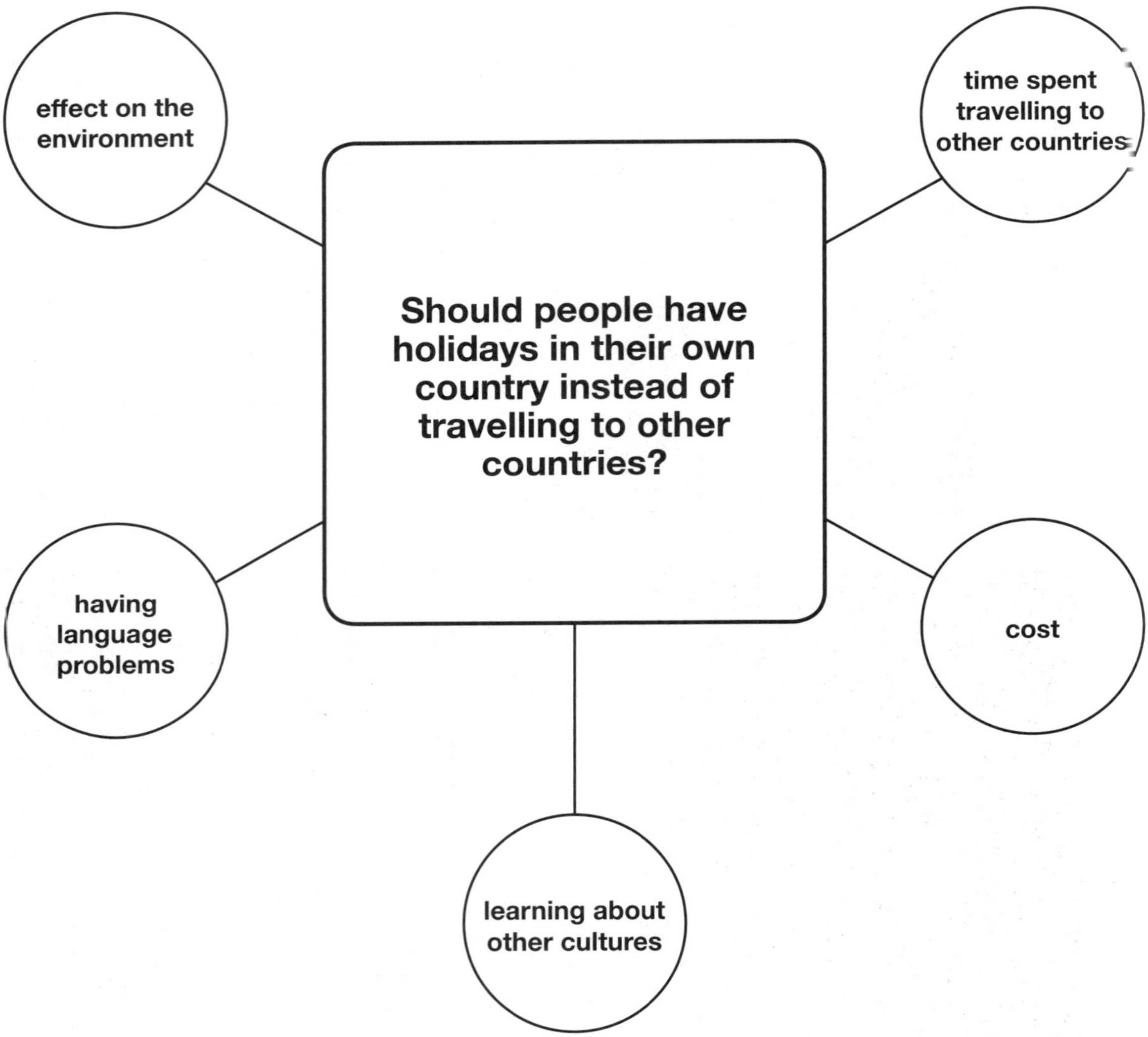
Should people have holidays in their own country instead of travelling to other countries?
effect on the environment
time spent travelling to other countries
having language problems
cost
learning about other cultures